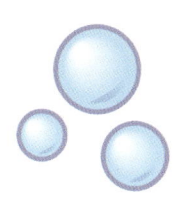

EXPLORING THE WORLD OF AQUATIC LIFE

VOLUME 3

Fan–Lio

Copyright © 2009 The Brown Reference Group plc

All rights reserved. No part of this book may be reproduced or utilized in any form or by any means, electronic or mechanical, including photocopying, recording, or by any information storage or retrieval systems, without permission in writing from the publisher. For information contact:

Chelsea House
An imprint of Infobase Publishing
132 West 31st Street
New York, NY 10001

Library of Congress Cataloging-in-Publication Data
Dawes, John, 1945–
Exploring the world of aquatic life / [consultant editor, John P. Friel; authors, John Dawes, Andrew Campbell].
     p. cm.
  Includes bibliographical references and index.
  ISBN 978-1-60413-255-7
 1. Aquatic biology--Juvenile literature. I. Campbell, Andrew. II. Friel, John P. III. Title.
  QH90.16.D39 2008
  591.77--dc22
                              2008030416

Chelsea House books are available at special discounts when purchased in bulk quantities for businesses, associations, institutions, or sales promotions. Please call our Special Sales Department in New York at (212) 967-8800 or (800) 322-8755.

You can find Chelsea House on the World Wide Web at
http://www.chelseahouse.com

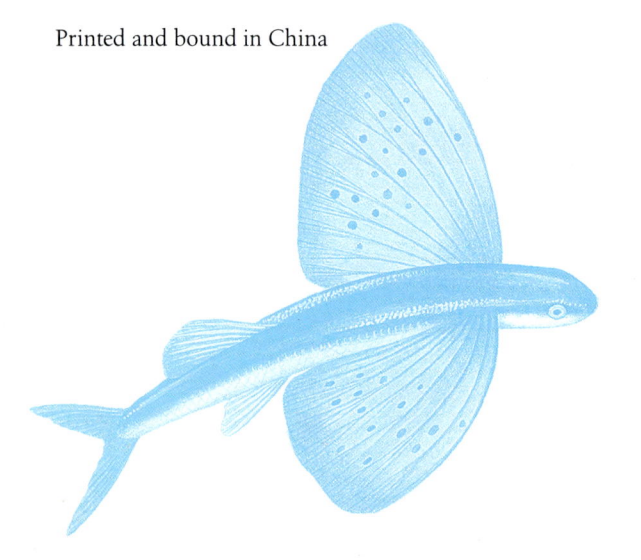

Printed and bound in China

For The Brown Reference Group plc
Project Editor: Graham Bateman
Editor: Derek Hall
Designers: Steve McCurdy, Tony Truscott
Design Manager: David Poole
Managing Editor: Miranda Smith
Editorial Director: Lindsey Lowe

Consultant Editor
John P. Friel, Ph.D.
Curator of Fishes, Amphibians & Reptiles
Cornell University Museum of Vertebrates
Ithaca, New York

Authors
John Dawes; Andrew Campbell

Picture Credits
FLPA: 10 Bruce Robison/Minden Pictures; 12 Brake/Sunset; 14 Reinhard Dirscherl/Bruce Coleman Inc; 16 R. Dirscherl; 18 Peter David; 19 Arthaud/Sunset; 22 Flip Nicklin/Minden Pictures; 24 Colin Marshall; 30 Sunset; 32 Konrad Wothe/Minden Pictures; 35 Hiroya Minakuchi/Minden Pictures; 36 Reinhard Dirscherl; 40 Wil Meinderts/Foto Natura; 42 Wil Meinderts/ Foto Natura; 44 David Hosking; 47 Derek Middleton; 48 Mark Jones/Minden Pictures; 50 Lacz Gerard/Sunset; 54 Norbert Wu/Minden Pictures; 56t Horizon Vision/Sunset; 56b Visage Albert/Sunset; 57 Flip Nicklin/Minden Pictures; 58 Silvestris Fotoservice; 62 R.Dirscherl; 63t Panda Photo; 63b Norbert Wu/Minden Pictures; 64 Flip Nicklin/Minden Pictures; 68 David Hosking; 70 D. P. Wilson. *Hippocampus Bildarchiv*: 66. *Photos.com*: 74b; 75. *Shutterstock*: 1 Dwight Smith; 20 Olga Bogatyrenko; 26 Yuyangc; 28 Parpalea Catalin; 29 Lim Tiaw Leong; 38 Loren Rodgers; 52 Frank B. Yuwono; 60 Dwight Smith; 72 Russell Swain; 74t Robert Pernell.

Artworks © The Brown Reference Group plc

The Brown Reference Group has made every effort to trace copyright holders of the pictures used in this book. Anyone having claims to ownership not identified above is invited to contact The Brown Reference Group.

CONTENTS

Introducing aquatic life	4
Invertebrate family tree	6
Fish and mammalian family tree	8
Fangtooths	10
Flying fish	12
Four-eyed fish	14
Freshwater eels	16
Frogfish	20
Garfish	22
Gobies	24
Goldfish	26
Gouramis	30
Gray whale	32
Great white shark	36
Grunion	38
Guppy	40
Hagfish and lampreys	44
Hammerhead sharks	48
Hatchetfish	50
Hermit crabs	52
Herring	54
Hydrozoans	58
Jellyfish	60
Krill	64
Lancelets	66
Leeches	68
Limpets	70
Lionfish, scorpionfish	72
Glossary	76
Further resources	79
Index	80

INTRODUCING AQUATIC LIFE

Life originated in the prehistoric seas some 4,000 million years ago. The watery habitats of today (oceans, rivers, and lakes) contain the most amazing and varied animal life to be found anywhere on Earth. It ranges in size from the huge blue whale—the biggest animal ever to have lived—to tiny creatures that can only be seen with a microscope. It also includes the many colorful fish and other sea creatures that live on coral reefs, as well as the barnacles, limpets, and winkles that cloak our rocky shores. Then there are the ferocious piranhas, the huge sturgeons, and other animals that live in our rivers and lakes. These, and many more, are the subjects of this encyclopedia.

Three quite different groups of animals are described in this set. **Invertebrates** are animals that do not have a backbone. Apart from that feature, all the major groups of invertebrates are very different from each other. Here we look at invertebrates that live in sea and fresh water, although other invertebrates include the land-dwelling insects and spiders. Most of the invertebrates in this set belong to four major phyla (groups): the jelly animals (such as the soft-bodied jellyfish and sea anemones); the crustaceans (such as the hard-skinned lobsters); the mollusks (such as the eight-limbed octopuses); and the spiny-skinned animals (such as the prickly sea urchins). We also include the mostly microscopic life forms that make up a group called the Protista, or single-celled life.

Fish are found all over the world in seas, oceans, rivers, and lakes. Fish are cold-blooded vertebrates (animals with backbones). Most have streamlined bodies covered in scales. They also have fins and a tail for swimming. Fish breathe with the aid of gills, but some also have lungs.

Finally there are those **mammals** that spend all their lives in the sea—the whales and dolphins, the dugong, and the manatees. Mammals are warm-blooded, air-breathing vertebrates that feed their young with milk.

Exploring the World of Aquatic Life

From the American paddlefish to wrasses, these six volumes of *Exploring the World of Aquatic Life* provide more than one hundred articles that describe in detail particular species and groups of animals that live in watery habitats. Most are articles about individual animals (such as the whale shark or the goldfish), or groups of closely related animals (such as sturgeons or barnacles). Other articles provide a general account of a large group of animals, such as crustaceans or sharks. They are shown in bold type on the table of contents in each volume.

Each volume has a number of useful features. At the front of each book there are two family trees; they show how these varied animals fit into the animal kingdom and how they are related to each another. They also give cross references to articles in this encyclopedia. At the end of each book there is a glossary of terms used throughout the set; a section entitled Further resources, which includes further reading and Internet resources; and a volume-specific index. Volume 6 contains a complete set index.

Every article has a Fact File box which summarizes the classification (see opposite) of each animal or group and indicates how many species exist. In addition, there are facts about the animals' distribution, habitat, size, coloration, diet, breeding, and status according to the World Conservation Union (IUCN; see opposite). Other items include boxes that provide more in-depth information about specific details and Did You Know? features that present interesting facts about specific animals. Throughout, there are large, colorful photographs and illustrations that increase the reader's enjoyment and enhance an understanding of those animals that live in watery habitats.

Group ties

Above the Fact File in most articles there is a colored tag. This indicates in which general group of animals the subject is placed.

INVERTEBRATES are all those animals that do not have a backbone. The majority of them are built of many cells. However, also included in this group are the most simple forms of life that exist as a single cell; they make up the kingdom Protista.

PRIMITIVE FISH covers a varied group that includes the remnants of the very earliest fish to evolve, as well as their living descendants. Some, such as the hagfish, have primitive skeletons but do not have jaws. Others, such as the coelacanth, have a primitive bony skeleton. This group includes the sea squirts and lancelets. These small creatures are the ancestors of those animals, such as the bony fish and the sea mammals, that have a true backbone.

CARTILAGINOUS FISH have a skeleton that is made of cartilage, a gristlelike substance much softer than bone. Sharks are the best-known types of cartilaginous fish.

ADVANCED BONY FISH, also known as teleosts, are the largest and most varied group of fish. Over 24,000 species are known today.

SEA MAMMALS includes the whales and dolphins as well as the dugong and the manatees.

- INVERTEBRATES
- PRIMITIVE FISH
- CARTILAGINOUS FISH
- ADVANCED BONY FISH
- SEA MAMMALS

World Conservation Union (IUCN)

The World Conservation Union (IUCN) is the world's largest and most important conservation network. Its mission is to help protect all living organisms and natural resources by highlighting those threatened with extinction and therefore promote their conservation.

An organism may be placed in one of the following categories in the *IUCN Red List of Threatened Species*:

- **Extinct**—there is no reasonable doubt that the last individual has died
- **Extinct in the wild**—an organism survives only in captivity, in cultivation, or as a population well outside its past range
- **Critically endangered**—facing an extremely high risk of extinction in the wild
- **Endangered**—facing a very high risk of extinction in the wild
- **Vulnerable**—facing a high risk of extinction in the wild
- **Near threatened**—likely to qualify for a threatened category in the near future
- **Least concern**—is not threatened
- **Data deficient**—inadequate information exists to make an assessment

The status of each mammal or group of mammals according to the IUCN is highlighted at the foot of the Fact File in every article.

Classifying animals

To talk about animals, we need names for the different kinds. An Atlantic salmon is one type of fish; all individuals look alike, can breed together, and produce young that look like themselves. This is the zoologist's definition of a species. Scientists use an internationally agreed system of naming animals so that it is possible for anyone in the world to know which animal is being described, whatever the language. The name for a species consists of a two-word name, usually in Latin or Greek. That of the Atlantic salmon is *Salmo salar*.

Scientists create family trees showing how one animal, or group of animals, is related to another. This is called classification. The largest group is the kingdom. The kingdom Animalia covers all animals. Between kingdom and species there are many other categories or groupings, indicating ever-closer relationships. The sequence for the Atlantic salmon is kingdom: Animalia; phylum: Chordata; subphylum: Vertebrata; superclass: Gnathostomata; grade: Osteichthyes; class: Actinopterygii; division: Teleostei; order: Salmoniformes; family: Salmonidae; genus: *Salmo*; species: *Salmo salar*. (See also page 78.)

INVERTEBRATE FAMILY TREE

SINGLE-CELLED LIFE (Kingdom Protista) → **Animals without a backbone—invertebrates** (Kingdom Animalia) → **PHYLA** include: **JELLY ANIMALS** (Cnidaria) **MOLLUSKS** (Mollusca) **SPINY-SKINNED ANIMALS** (Echinodermata) **CRUSTACEANS** (Phylum Arthropoda: Subphylum Crustacea)

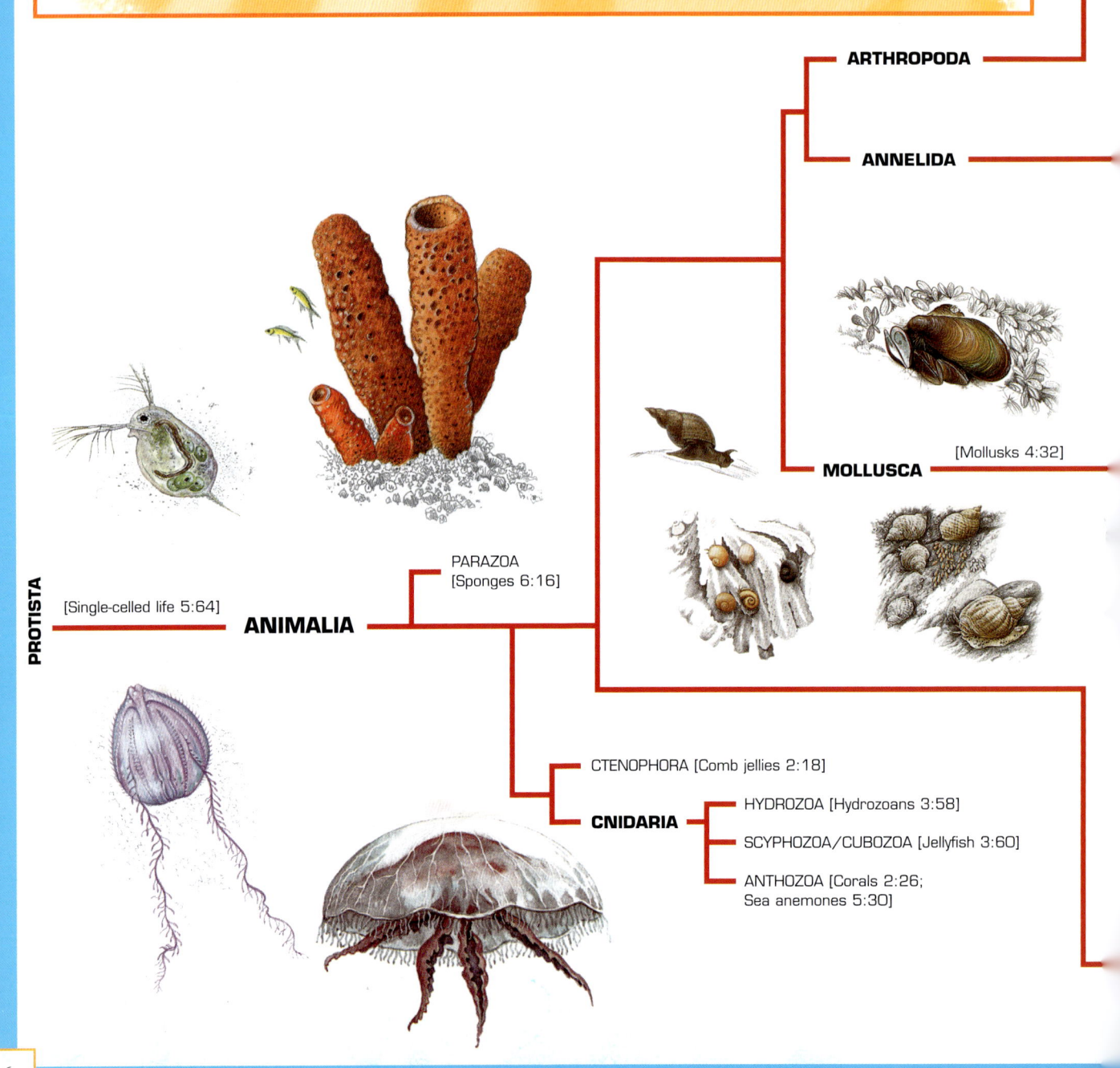

The numbers below refer to volume and page numbers where a particular group is featured in an article.

- ARTHROPODA
- ANNELIDA
- MOLLUSCA [Mollusks 4:32]
- PARAZOA [Sponges 6:16]
- PROTISTA [Single-celled life 5:64]
- ANIMALIA
- CTENOPHORA [Comb jellies 2:18]
- CNIDARIA
  - HYDROZOA [Hydrozoans 3:58]
  - SCYPHOZOA/CUBOZOA [Jellyfish 3:60]
  - ANTHOZOA [Corals 2:26; Sea anemones 5:30]

- Spiders/insects and allies
- **CRUSTACEA** [Crustaceans 2:36]
  - BRANCHIOPODA [Water fleas 6:54]
  - MAXILLOPODA [Barnacles 1:36]
  - **MALACOSTRACA**
    - STOMATOPODA [Mantis shrimp 4:22]
    - AMPHIPODA [Sand hoppers 5:26]
    - EUPHAUSIACEA [Krill 3:64]
    - **DECAPODA**
      - BRACHYURA [Crabs 2:30]
      - ASTACIDEA [Lobsters and crayfish 4:12]
      - PENAEIDEA, CARIDEA, STENOPODIDEA [Shrimp and prawns 5:58]
      - ANOMURA [Hermit crabs 3:52; Squat lobsters 6:18]

- POGONOPHORA [Beard worms 1:42]
- POLYCHAETA [Ragworms and allies 5:10]
- HIRUDINEA [Leeches 3:68]

- **GASTROPODA**
  - ARCHAEOGASTROPODA [Limpets 3:70]
  - MESOGASTROPODA [Winkles and relatives 6:66]
  - NEOGASTROPODA [Whelks and relatives 6:64]
  - NUDIBRANCHIA [Sea slugs 5:44]

- **BIVALVIA**
  - DYSODONTA [Mussels 4:44]
  - OSTREIFORMES [Oysters 4:54]
  - PSEUDOLAMELLIBRANCHIATA [Scallops 5:28]
  - EULAMELLIBRANCHIA [Cockles and clams 2:10]

- **CEPHALOPODA**
  - NAUTILOIDEA [Nautiluses 4:48]
  - **COLEOIDEA**
    - **OCTOPODIFORMES** — OCTOPODA [Octopuses 4:50]
    - **DECAPODIFORMES**
      - SEPIIDA [Cuttlefish 2:42]
      - SPIRULIDA, SEPIOLIDA, TEUTHIDA [Squid 6:20]

- **ECHINODERMATA** [Spiny-skinned animals 6:14]
  - CRINOIDEA [Sea lilies 5:42]
  - ASTEROIDEA/OPHIUROIDEA [Starfish 6:24]
  - ECHINOIDEA [Sea urchins 5:48]
  - HOLOTHUROIDEA [Sea cucumbers 5:36]

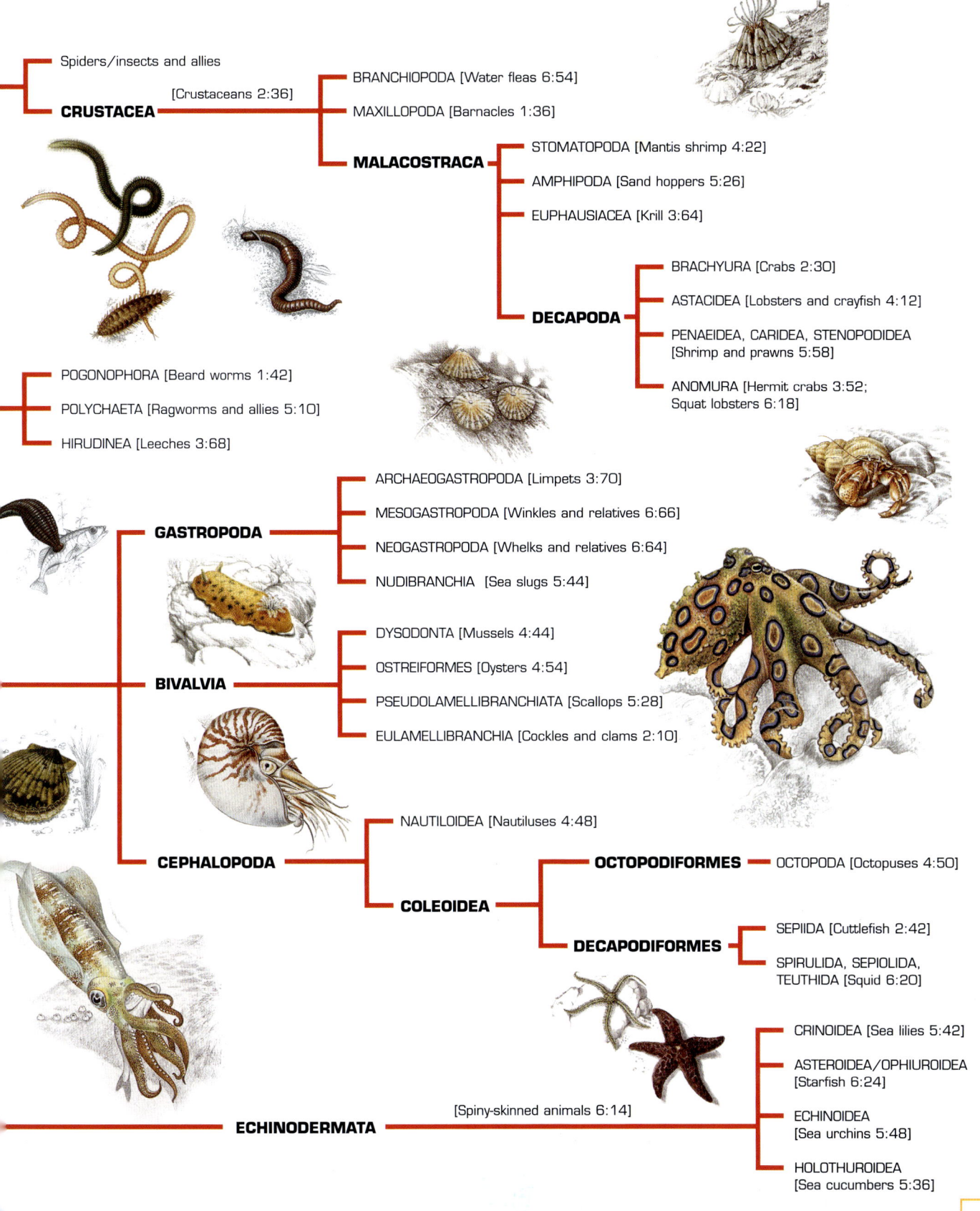

7

FISH AND MAMMALIAN FAMILY TREE

ANIMALS (Kingdom Animalia)
→ **Animals without a true backbone (primitive vertebrates)** (Phylum Chordata: Subphylum Urochordata —**SEA SQUIRTS**; Subphylum Cephalochordata —**LANCELETS**)
→ **Animals with a backbone** (Phylum Chordata: Subphylum Vertebrata)

MAIN GROUPS:
MAMMALS (Class Mammalia)
BIRDS (Class Aves)
REPTILES (Class Reptilia)
AMPHIBIANS (Class Amphibia)
HAGFISH, LAMPREYS (Superclass Agnatha)
CARTILAGINOUS FISH (Class Chondrichthyes)
LOBE-FINNED BONY FISH (Class Sarcopterygii)
RAY-FINNED BONY FISH (Class Actinopterygii)

The numbers below refer to volume and page numbers where a particular group is featured in an article.

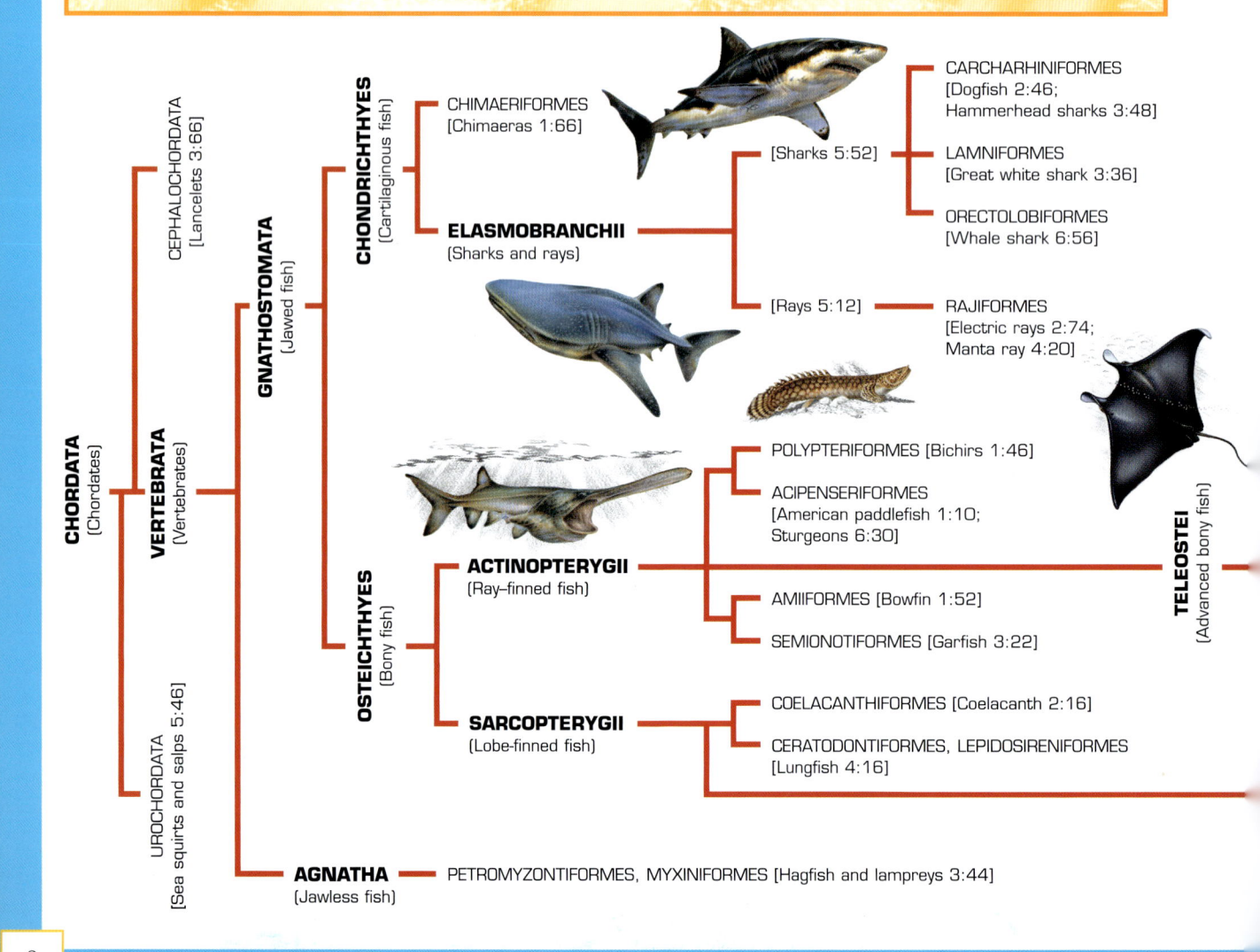

CHORDATA (Chordates)
- **UROCHORDATA** [Sea squirts and salps 5:46]
- **VERTEBRATA** (Vertebrates)
  - **CEPHALOCHORDATA** [Lancelets 3:66]
  - **GNATHOSTOMATA** (Jawed fish)
    - **CHONDRICHTHYES** (Cartilaginous fish)
      - CHIMAERIFORMES [Chimaeras 1:66]
      - **ELASMOBRANCHII** (Sharks and rays)
        - [Sharks 5:52]
          - CARCHARHINIFORMES [Dogfish 2:46; Hammerhead sharks 3:48]
          - LAMNIFORMES [Great white shark 3:36]
          - ORECTOLOBIFORMES [Whale shark 6:56]
        - [Rays 5:12]
          - RAJIFORMES [Electric rays 2:74; Manta ray 4:20]
    - **OSTEICHTHYES** (Bony fish)
      - **ACTINOPTERYGII** (Ray-finned fish)
        - POLYPTERIFORMES [Bichirs 1:46]
        - ACIPENSERIFORMES [American paddlefish 1:10; Sturgeons 6:30]
        - **TELEOSTEI** (Advanced bony fish)
        - AMIIFORMES [Bowfin 1:52]
        - SEMIONOTIFORMES [Garfish 3:22]
      - **SARCOPTERYGII** (Lobe-finned fish)
        - COELACANTHIFORMES [Coelacanth 2:16]
        - CERATODONTIFORMES, LEPIDOSIRENIFORMES [Lungfish 4:16]
  - **AGNATHA** (Jawless fish) — PETROMYZONTIFORMES, MYXINIFORMES [Hagfish and lampreys 3:44]

8

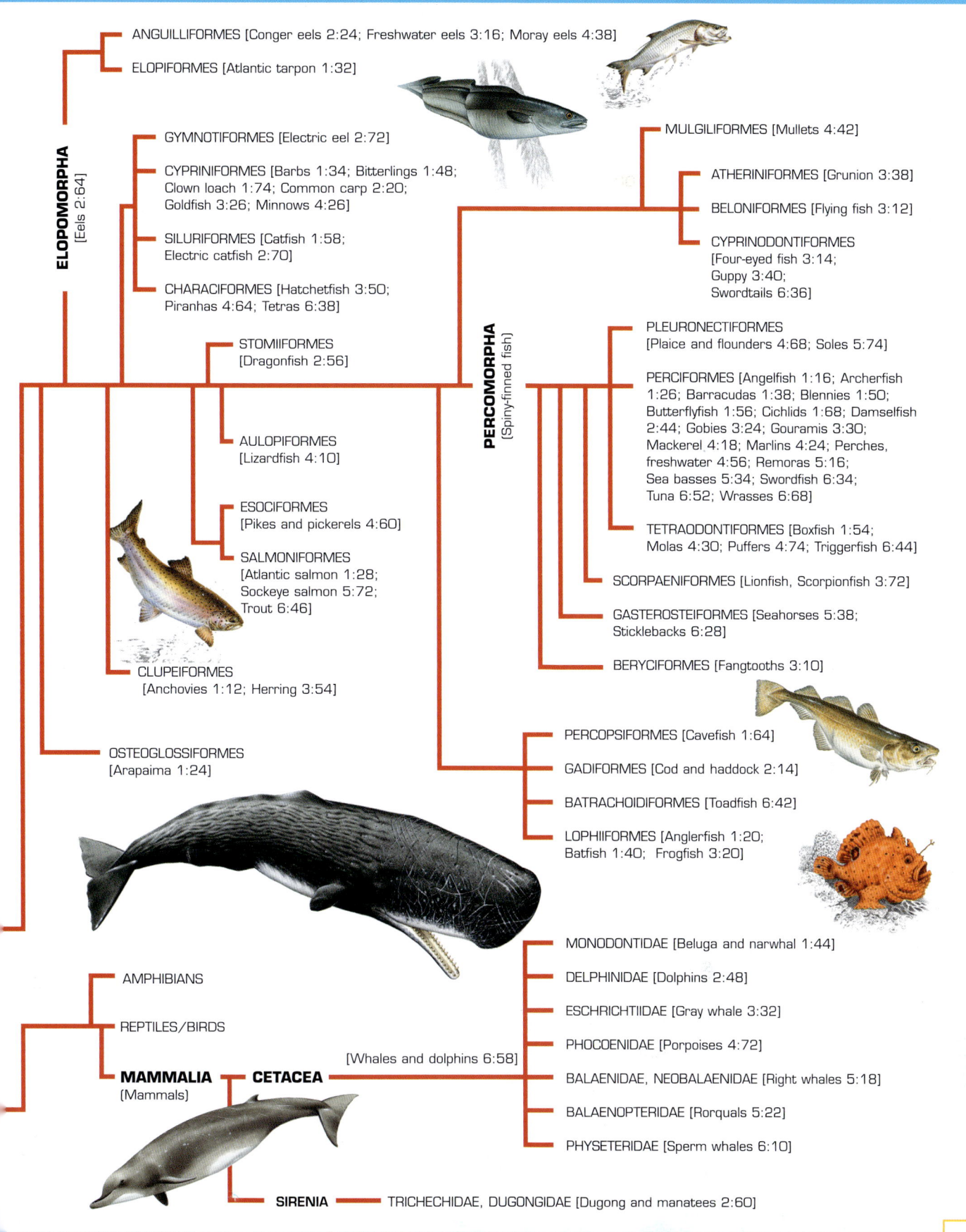

ELOPOMORPHA [Eels 2:64]
- ANGUILLIFORMES [Conger eels 2:24; Freshwater eels 3:16; Moray eels 4:38]
- ELOPIFORMES [Atlantic tarpon 1:32]

- GYMNOTIFORMES [Electric eel 2:72]
- CYPRINIFORMES [Barbs 1:34; Bitterlings 1:48; Clown loach 1:74; Common carp 2:20; Goldfish 3:26; Minnows 4:26]
- SILURIFORMES [Catfish 1:58; Electric catfish 2:70]
- CHARACIFORMES [Hatchetfish 3:50; Piranhas 4:64; Tetras 6:38]

- STOMIIFORMES [Dragonfish 2:56]

PERCOMORPHA (Spiny-finned fish)
- MULGILIFORMES [Mullets 4:42]
- ATHERINIFORMES [Grunion 3:38]
- BELONIFORMES [Flying fish 3:12]
- CYPRINODONTIFORMES [Four-eyed fish 3:14; Guppy 3:40; Swordtails 6:36]
- PLEURONECTIFORMES [Plaice and flounders 4:68; Soles 5:74]
- PERCIFORMES [Angelfish 1:16; Archerfish 1:26; Barracudas 1:38; Blennies 1:50; Butterflyfish 1:56; Cichlids 1:68; Damselfish 2:44; Gobies 3:24; Gouramis 3:30; Mackerel 4:18; Marlins 4:24; Perches, freshwater 4:56; Remoras 5:16; Sea basses 5:34; Swordfish 6:34; Tuna 6:52; Wrasses 6:68]
- TETRAODONTIFORMES [Boxfish 1:54; Molas 4:30; Puffers 4:74; Triggerfish 6:44]
- SCORPAENIFORMES [Lionfish, Scorpionfish 3:72]
- GASTEROSTEIFORMES [Seahorses 5:38; Sticklebacks 6:28]
- BERYCIFORMES [Fangtooths 3:10]

- AULOPIFORMES [Lizardfish 4:10]
- ESOCIFORMES [Pikes and pickerels 4:60]
- SALMONIFORMES [Atlantic salmon 1:28; Sockeye salmon 5:72; Trout 6:46]
- CLUPEIFORMES [Anchovies 1:12; Herring 3:54]

- PERCOPSIFORMES [Cavefish 1:64]
- GADIFORMES [Cod and haddock 2:14]
- BATRACHOIDIFORMES [Toadfish 6:42]
- LOPHIIFORMES [Anglerfish 1:20; Batfish 1:40; Frogfish 3:20]

- OSTEOGLOSSIFORMES [Arapaima 1:24]

- AMPHIBIANS
- REPTILES/BIRDS

MAMMALIA (Mammals)

CETACEA [Whales and dolphins 6:58]
- MONODONTIDAE [Beluga and narwhal 1:44]
- DELPHINIDAE [Dolphins 2:48]
- ESCHRICHTIIDAE [Gray whale 3:32]
- PHOCOENIDAE [Porpoises 4:72]
- BALAENIDAE, NEOBALAENIDAE [Right whales 5:18]
- BALAENOPTERIDAE [Rorquals 5:22]
- PHYSETERIDAE [Sperm whales 6:10]

SIRENIA — TRICHECHIDAE, DUGONGIDAE [Dugong and manatees 2:60]

9

FANGTOOTHS

These voracious marine hunters have fearsome, sharp fangs and especially large mouths. Once seized, there is no escape for any unfortunate victim targeted by a fangtooth.

ADVANCED BONY FISH

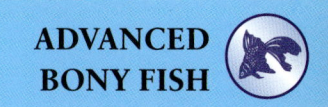

For all their reputation as deadly hunters of the deep, fangtooths are small fish that can themselves fall victim to larger hunters like tuna and marlin. Against such large predators, fangtooths have little defense. However, their hard, bony body gives them protection from many other smaller hunters. This hard body is an unusual feature in deep-sea fish, which normally have soft, flexible bodies, despite the high pressures experienced at great depths.

Young fangtooths also carry protection against predators in the form of a spine on top of the head and another on the bottom edge of one of the bones that cover the gills. Baby fangtooths look so different from adults that, for about a hundred years, they were each thought to belong to separate species.

Deadly Combination

Sharp teeth, large mouths, and (often) large stomachs are commonly found in deepwater predators. This combination allows such fish to survive in an environment where food is scarce. If a suitable meal comes along, no hunter can afford to let the opportunity swim away. It could be a long time before another meal happens to come within reach.

Not surprisingly, therefore, deepwater hunters like fangtooths have mouths and teeth designed to grab hold of such prey and swallow it whole—even if at first the meal appears to be too large to swallow.

Fangtooths are adapted to grab any potential meal. However, the widely spaced teeth are not suited to cutting food up, so any prey is swallowed whole.

Fact File

FANGTOOTHS

Family: Anoplogastridae (2 species)
Order: Beryciformes

Where do they live?: Common fangtooth: worldwide in deep tropical and temperate seas; shorthorn fangtooth: tropical Pacific and Atlantic Oceans

Habitat: Deep water: common fangtooth is found between 1,640–16,400 feet (500–5,000 m); shorthorn fangtooth is found in shallower water: 3,300–4,920 feet (1,000–1,500 m)

Size: Common fangtooth up to 7 inches (18 cm); shorthorn fangtooth just over 2.4 inches (6 cm)

Coloration: Deep brown to black

Diet: Fish (mainly) and shellfish

Breeding: Eggs and sperm are released into the water and float to the surface; the young spend some time among the plankton

Status: Not known to be threatened

FLYING FISH

Some fish blend in with their background, or huddle together to form large, tight balls of writhing bodies to escape from hunters, but flying fish can quite simply disappear from view.

ADVANCED BONY FISH

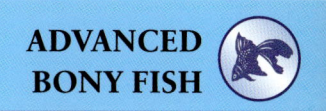

It must be disconcerting for a hunter to discover that the prey it is chasing suddenly disappears. Yet, this is precisely what happens when flying fish are being pursued. When they sense danger, flying fish break through the water surface and put on a burst of speed using lightning-fast beats of their specially adapted tail—it can beat at up to fifty times per second! Once flying fish reach take-off speed, which can be around 37 miles per hour, they leave the water completely and glide above the surface on their highly modified winglike pectoral (chest) fins.

Gliders or Flyers?

To see a shoal of flying fish taking off and gliding over the water surface on a calm day is an unforgettable experience. From a distance, they look more like a flock of seabirds skimming the waves than a shoal of fish.

Although we call them flying fish, these fish are gliders rather than flyers. They do not flap their wings in the way that animals do when in true flight. Flying fish merely hold their pectoral fins at 90 degrees to their body and glide. The distances covered can be considerable, however. Just how far a flying fish glides depends on the severity of the threat, on wind speed, on the size of the individual, and on the species. The distance can range up to 80 feet in species that have the normal two "wings" and up to 650 feet in those that also possess winglike pelvic (hip) fins.

A group of flying fish takes to the air in an attempt to escape from an unseen predator, such as a tuna or a swordfish, in the waters below.

Fact File

FLYING FISH

Family: Exocoetidae (about 67 species)

Order: Beloniformes

Where do they live?: Most tropical and temperate seas

Habitat: Usually remain relatively close to the water surface

Size: From around 5.5 inches (14 cm) in the African sailfin flying fish to 20 inches (50 cm) in *Chelopogon pinnatibarbatus japonicus*

Coloration: Most species have deep blue coloration on the back, shading into lighter colors along the sides and silvery along the belly

Diet: Mainly plankton

Breeding: Some species spawn among mats of floating seaweeds; the eggs, which float, are abandoned

Status: Not known to be threatened

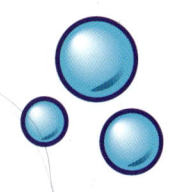

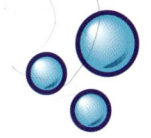

FOUR-EYED FISH

Four-eyed fish are not brightly colored, nor do they have elaborate fins. In fact, they look just like ordinary fish—except that they have the most incredible eyes.

ADVANCED BONY FISH

As their name indicates, these cylinderlike fish have four eyes. At least, they give the impression of having four eyes. On closer examination, however, it can be seen that in fact they only have two eyes, just like most other fish. However, each eye has two colored strips of tissue that extend inward from the iris and meet in the center of the pupil. This effectively divides each eye into a top half and a bottom half, creating the illusion of four, instead of two, eyes.

Two-way Vision

This division is accompanied by changes to the lens inside the eye. These give four-eyed fish the ability to see above and below the water surface at the same time. The secret of this ability lies in the shape of the lens. Animals that live surrounded by air, rather than water, have long, slim eye lenses with the sides slightly curved outward. This is known as a convex shape and is the best one for seeing in air. However, the best shape for seeing under water is spherical.

The lenses in the eyes of four-eyed fish have both shapes: slightly convex sides facing upward into the air, and rounded ends facing the water. Inside each eye there are two retinas (the layers of tissue that receive images and pass them to the brain, allowing animals to see). One receives images from the air and the other gets images from the water. This gives the fish a unique and extraordinary ability.

The unusual structure of the eyes of four-eyed fish is shown here. Another surprising feature of these fish is their ability to survive out of water at low tide.

Fact File

FOUR-EYED FISH

Subfamily: Anablepinae (3 species)
Family: Anablepidae
Order: Cyprinodontiformes

Where do they live?: South America

Habitat: Found in fresh water and estuaries, almost entirely near the surface, with the top half of each eye exposed to the air

Size: From around 8.7 inches (22 cm) in the Pacific four-eyed fish to around 12 inches (30 cm) in the large-scale foureyes and the finescaled foureyes

Coloration: Drab, light-brownish on the back, fading to a white belly

Diet: Small fish, invertebrates, and vegetation

Breeding: Eggs are fertilized inside the body of the female, which subsequently gives birth to fully formed young

Status: Not known to be threatened

15

FRESHWATER EELS

From willow-leaved larvae to snakelike adults, eels have fascinated and mystified us for centuries. Even today, they still have many secrets, some of which we may never uncover.

ADVANCED BONY FISH

The amazing story of European and American eels begins, not in the rivers where the adults are found, but in deep water in part of the western Atlantic known as the Sargasso Sea. In the case of the European eel, this is some 4,000 miles away from the home rivers of the adults. Larval eels (known as leptocephali) take up to three years to cover the distance from their place of birth to their eventual homes. For the American eel, the journey is much shorter, but it can still take the larvae about a year to complete the trip.

Mysterious Origins

Eels have been steeped in mystery for many centuries. For example, the ancient Greek writer Aristotle believed that eels, which have slimy bodies, were actually formed from slime. He also believed that baby eels arose from "the entrails [bowels] of the earth." Another Greek writer, Pliny, believed that baby eels were formed from pieces of the skin of adult eels scraped off by rocks. In the eighteenth century, there was a widely held belief that eels arose from the hairs of horses' tails. A century later, it was claimed that a particular beetle gave birth to baby eels.

Many eel mysteries still remain today. For example, although scientists know that American and European eels breed in the Sargasso Sea, no adults have ever been caught in the area. Amazingly, no eel eggs have ever been collected in the Sargasso Sea either.

A European eel swims along the river bed. When ready to breed, an eel will even travel over land at night in its determination to reach the sea.

Fact File

FRESHWATER EELS

Family: Anguillidae (around 20 species)

Order: Anguilliformes

Where do they live?: Eastern North America to northern South America, and much of Europe

Habitat: Young hatch and spend time at sea; adults live in fresh water

Size: From around 27.5 inches–6.6 feet (70 cm–2 m); but up to 4.9 feet (1.5 m) in the American eel and 4.3 feet (1.3 m) in the European eel

Coloration: Grayish-brown along the back, changing to yellow along the belly; belly becomes white when adult and upper parts darken

Diet: Feeding occurs in fresh water: invertebrates and fish are taken

Breeding: Thought to occur in deep warm water—probably down to 15,000 feet (4,500 m) in some species; American and European eels spawn in the Sargasso Sea; a large female can release up to 20 million eggs which hatch in about 48 hours; larvae (leptocephali) drift in the sea for an extended period of time before they reach their home coasts

Status: Not known to be threatened

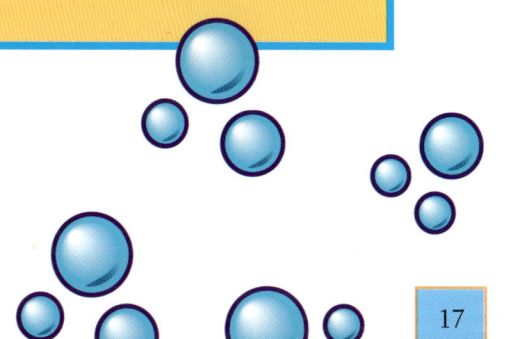

FRESHWATER EELS

From Leptocephalus to Eel

So how do adult eels find their way from their home rivers to the Sargasso, especially when they are such weak swimmers? Also, how can the larvae survive for two or three years without food, yet still manage to grow? (No food has ever been found in the guts of larval eels.) When young eels appear off the American and European coasts, they are already about 6 inches long. Yet, why are no smaller eels ever found?

In fact, the answers to these questions have been available since 1783. It was in that year that a transparent, leaflike fish was collected, described, and given the name "leptocephalus." About 130 years later, two other leptocephali were caught. This time, they were kept alive in an aquarium. Over a period of time, they changed into the familiar shape of the adult eels. At that point, it was realized that leptocephali were not separate species but, quite simply, eel larvae.

The leaflike leptocephalus larva of an eel.

Breeding Grounds

Although countless millions of eels had been caught, gutted, and eaten

DID YOU KNOW?

- Although they do not feed, larval eels have forward-pointing teeth.
- All twenty or so species of eel are believed to spawn in warm waters, probably at depths of between 600–15,000 feet.
- Eel blood contains a dangerous poison, but it is destroyed by cooking.

ADVANCED BONY FISH

over the centuries, none was ever found with egg-filled ovaries, or ripe eggs, or even sperm inside them. The first of these discoveries had to wait until 1777, when developing ovaries were found in a female specimen. About a hundred years later, a mature male was found, followed, several years on, by a fully mature female.

It had nevertheless been observed that at certain times of the year adult eels showed an irresistible drive to reach the sea, even slithering over damp ground to do so. Gradually, it was realized that eels bred at sea.

After the leptocephali were discovered, a search was mounted to trace them back to their place of birth. Their size, and the location where leptocephali were collected, were recorded and a remarkable picture began to emerge. It was realized that the smallest leptocephali occurred in the Sargasso Sea and that it was here that adult eels spawned.

Eels up to two years of age are called elvers or glass eels.

FINDING THE SARGASSO SEA

How do young eels, that have never even entered the sea before, travel unerringly over thousands of miles to find the Sargasso Sea? Perhaps they are guided by a rise in water temperature? But this could not help those eels that migrate from the Mediterranean, since this sea is as warm as the Sargasso itself. Could changes in the saltiness of the water guide them? Probably not, since eels do not seem to be affected by whether salt is present in the water or not. Finally, it has been suggested that they might follow the Earth's magnetic field. But this also seems unlikely, because no organ has been found in eels that can detect magnetic fields. The eels' method of navigation remains a mystery so far.

FROGFISH

Some look like sponges, while others mimic algae-covered stones. Some even look just like seaweed—but no seaweed swallows victims in less than one-hundredth of a second!

ADVANCED BONY FISH

Frogfish are close relatives of anglerfish, with which they share a number of characteristics. The most obvious of these is that they carry their own angling equipment in the form of a "rod and lure."

The rod consists of the first ray of the dorsal (back) fin while the lure, or bait, is a fleshy bit at the end that is used to attract prey. In the warty frogfish this lure not only looks like a fish, but is actually moved through the water as if it were a small swimming fish.

Master Hunters

Apart from the Sargassum frogfish, frogfish are very poor swimmers. They spend their time on the bottom or "'walking" over it using the pectoral (chest) and pelvic (hip) fins, which are muscular and can be moved like limbs. These allow frogfish to move around in search of a suitable hunting spot, undetected both by their prey and their own predators.

With their rod and lure, and some of the best camouflage in the fish world, it is hardly surprising that frogfish are such successful hunters. Some species can even change color over a period of hours to match their surroundings. In the case of the Sargassum frogfish, the body is mottled in such a way, and in such colors, that it blends in perfectly with the Sargassum seaweed in which it lives. It is therefore very difficult for a potential victim to spot this fish, even if it is only an inch or so away—by which time it is far too late.

Resembling little more than the colorful marine growths among which it conceals itself, a frogfish lies in wait for unsuspecting prey.

Fact File

FROGFISH

Family: Antennariidae (over 40 species)

Order: Lophiiformes

Where do they live?: Widespread in tropical and subtropical oceans and seas around the world

Habitat: Vast majority of species live on the bottom in shallow or relatively shallow water; the Sargassum frogfish lives among Sargassum seaweed; the Indo-Australian brackish water frogfish occasionally enters estuaries

Size: Many species measure 1–2 inches (2.5–5 cm); the largest species, the roughbar frogfish, can measure over 13 inches (33 cm)

Coloration: Extremely variable, often colorful—like the sponges, seaweeds, and encrusted rocks among which they live

Diet: Smaller fish and invertebrates; may also eat each other

Breeding: Eggs are laid covered in a jellylike substance, and are released close to the surface where they are abandoned in most species; in some, the eggs may remain attached to the body of the male for a time

Status: Not known to be threatened

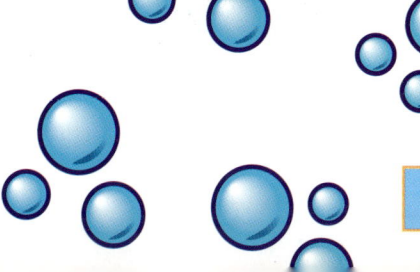

GARFISH

The southern parts of the United States and Mexico are home to a fish that not only eats others of its own kind but also feeds on birds and alligators. There are also reports that it attacks humans.

ADVANCED BONY FISH

The fish with the formidable reputation described opposite is the alligator gar. However, its name has nothing to do with an account in a book published in 1820 that tells of a fight between an alligator gar and an alligator. It ended with the gar cutting the alligator in two and swallowing it. The name actually comes from the fish's broad snout that gives the head an alligatorlike shape when it is viewed from above.

The attacks on humans are unconfirmed. However, there is no doubt that this species of gar is large enough, powerful enough, and sufficiently aggressive to mount such an attack.

Ancient Hunters

Gars are perfectly "built for the kill," with their long, cylinderlike, powerful bodies. Their long snouts are armed with numerous pointed teeth, and they have acute hunters' instincts. These characteristics have evolved over millions of years. The first gars probably appeared on Earth some 175–145 million years ago. They were widely distributed and ranged over North, Central, and South America, as well as Europe, Africa, and India—and possibly other places as well.

There have, therefore, been gars in American waters for a very long time. They are highly prized, primarily as game fish, although they are also eaten. The eggs of some gars are poisonous, however, and must be carefully removed prior to cooking.

In the southern United States the alligator gar (shown left) and the longnose gar are fished on a commercial scale, since the flesh of both these species is prized.

Fact File

GARFISH

Family: Lepisosteidae (7 species)

Order: Semionotiformes

Where do they live?: Central America, Cuba, and North America as far north as the Great Lakes

Habitat: Still or slow-flowing waters of large rivers, pools, lakes, and swamps, often containing submerged branches and vegetation; some species may enter estuaries

Size: From around 33 inches (84 cm) in the shortnose gar to around 10 feet (3 m) in the case of the alligator gar

Coloration: Brownish or other dark colors, accompanied by mottling along the back; lighter sides and belly

Diet: Mainly fish, crustaceans, and waterbirds

Breeding: Often occurs in groups in shallow warm water, either over vegetation or in a depression dug out by the female, depending on species; up to 77,000 eggs may be laid and hatch out between 6–9 days later

Status: Not known to be threatened

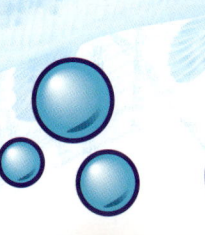

GOBIES

From record breakers to species with very unusual habits, gobies are among the most widespread and varied of all fish. Gobies also include some critically endangered species.

ADVANCED BONY FISH

The male of the freshwater dwarf pygmy goby is just 0.4 inches long. A marine goby, known as *Trimmatom nanus*, is even smaller at 0.39 inches, while several others are only slightly larger.

It is only since the early 2000s that the goby world record for the smallest vertebrate (animal with a backbone) on the planet has been beaten—by another fish, a relative of the carp known as *Paedocypris*, that only reaches a length of 0.3 inches. Not all gobies are tiny, though. Some, such as the violet goby, are relatively large and can grow to more than 22 inches in length.

Varied Family

There are many different species in the family, and gobies are extremely varied in their habits. For example, mudskippers do as their name suggests. They skip over the mud at low tide in the mangroves where they live. They come out of the water to feed and display to each other on the exposed mudflats.

Other gobies share burrows with a species of shrimp. The burrow is dug out by the shrimp, which benefits from the association because the goby raises the alarm when any predator approaches. The gobies, for their part, get protection because they are able to dive into the burrows at the first sign of danger. The sponge goby also dives for cover when threatened—right into the body cavity of a loggerhead sponge. There are even some gobies that climb waterfalls!

The mottled coloration of this banded flaphead goby, seen in the waters off Sulawesi, Indonesia, helps it blend in superbly with the seabed.

Fact File

GOBIES

Family: Gobiidae (around 2,000 species)

Order: Perciformes

Where do they live?: Widely distributed in tropical and temperate regions; only a few species live in cooler waters

Habitat: Most are found in brackish (slightly salty) or marine conditions, but some are also found in fresh water; several species form partnerships with other creatures

Size: From around 0.39–28 inches (9.9 mm–71 cm), but most species are 3–8 inches (8–20 cm) long

Coloration: Extremely variable; some bottom-dwelling species are well camouflaged, while others are brilliantly colored

Diet: Most feed on invertebrates; some feed on plankton; larger species may also feed on small fish

Breeding: Eggs are usually laid on a carefully prepared site, such as a rock or the roof of a cave, and are guarded by the male

Status: 25 species are listed as being under serious threat; some, like the dwarf pygmy goby, are critically endangered

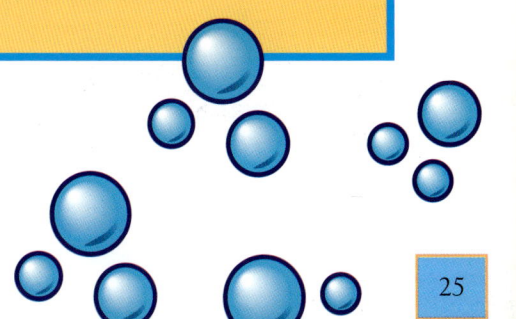

GOLDFISH

It has no scales on its head and is toothless. It does not even have a proper stomach. Yet, despite such apparent disadvantages, the goldfish is still the most widely kept pet in the world.

ADVANCED BONY FISH

The goldfish is a close relative of the common carp and, like its cousin, it lacks scales on the top of its head. As a result, the goldfish has been referred to as being bald. Also, in keeping with its closest relations, the goldfish has no teeth in its jaws. However, it does have grinding teeth in its throat.

Another peculiarity of the goldfish is its gut. While it is very long—a feature typical of fish whose diet is made up largely of plant matter—it does not have a separate stomach. In reality, of course, these are not disadvantages. They are simply characteristics of a species that is highly successful and perfectly adapted to its particular way of life in the wild.

Fish of Many Colors

Another feature that is typical of wild goldfish is that they are olive-brown in color. This helps them blend in with their background—usually muddy bottoms with waterweeds—and offers protection from predators. Other colors, such as yellow or orange, are also seen in wild goldfish, but these are relatively rare.

The many colors of the varieties of goldfish kept as popular pets worldwide have been developed through careful breeding over the centuries. For example, it is reported that several red-scaled fish were first seen in China between CE 265 and 316—over 1,740 years ago. We do not have firm proof of this, but the first definite reports are between 730 and 1,050 years old.

The immense popularity of goldfish worldwide has resulted in people breeding them in an ever-wider range of colors and in different body and fin shapes.

Fact File

GOLDFISH

Carassius auratus
Family: Cyprinidae
Order: Cypriniformes

Where do they live?: Originally found in Central Asia, China, and Japan, but introduced to most parts of the world

Habitat: Wide range of waters, including lakes, rivers, and ditches; still or slow-flowing waters are preferred, particularly those with soft clay and mud on the bottom

Size: Up to 23.2 inches (59 cm) but generally smaller; some specimens can grow larger in captivity

Coloration: Mainly olive-brown to olive-green, but silver, yellow, gold, and other colors are also known in wild populations; bred varieties come in a wide range of colors

Diet: Wide-ranging, including vegetation and small invertebrates

Breeding: Many thousands of sticky eggs are released among vegetation in spring; hatching can take up to 1 week, depending on temperature; eggs may develop without fertilization in some races

Status: Not known to be under threat

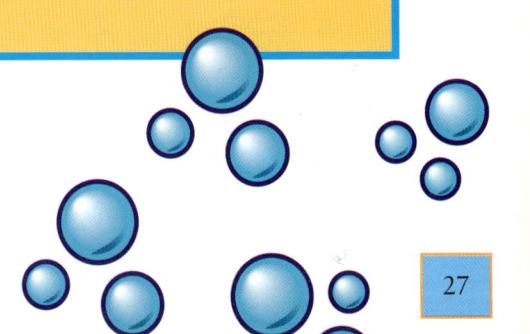

GOLDFISH

Since then, goldfish have been bred in a range of colors that includes white, black, brown, red, orange, yellow, and blue—with all shades in between. Breeding an animal or plant to produce a particular feature—such as color—is called selective breeding.

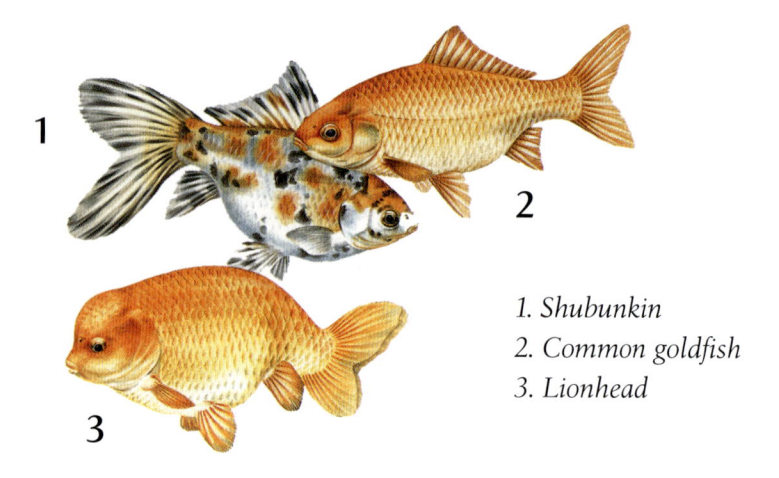

Many Shapes

As well as breeding goldfish of different colors, fishkeepers have also bred goldfish with unusual heads, body shapes, eyes, scales, fins, and nostrils. For example, there are goldfish with large bubblelike eyes, or with large eyes that are forever directed upward. Others have raspberrylike growths on their head and/or cheeks, two "bubbles" on their head, or pom-pomlike nostrils.. Yet more have double fins, maybe lack a back (dorsal) fin altogether, have long flowing fins, or short stubby fins.

1. Shubunkin
2. Common goldfish
3. Lionhead

Some varieties have short egg-shaped bodies, scales that stand out like pearls, or even scaleless, shiny, or matt (non-shiny) bodies.

All of these features can occur in any combination, with the result that there are well over one hundred varieties of goldfish officially recognized today. Selective breeding

▼ The veiltail is an attractive type of ornamental goldfish with long, flowing fins.

DID YOU KNOW?

- The longest cultivated goldfish ever recorded are over 18 inches long.
- The first official importation of the goldfish into America occurred in 1870.
- Goldfish eggs can sometimes develop without being fertilized.

ADVANCED BONY FISH

continues, and new varieties of goldfish appear regularly, particularly in Far Eastern countries where there is great interest in breeding these fish.

Breeding Pimples

In the breeding season, male goldfish develop small, white, pimplelike growths (known as nuptial tubercles). These appear on their snout (nose), cheeks, gill covers, and the front edge of the pectoral (chest) fins. In some individuals, the growths can also extend to the top of the head and along the back.

While these growths may have a number of uses about which we are unsure, there is one that we have a good idea about. The body of a goldfish is covered in a layer of protective, slimelike mucus that makes these fish rather slippery. The rough texture of the growths may therefore help a male to keep in close body contact with the slippery female during spawning, when sperm and eggs are released.

The growths on the cheeks and pectoral fins would be particularly useful for this purpose. Those on the snout could, perhaps, also help the male encourage the female during spawning, or even repel rival males.

Since the male's tubercles disappear once the breeding season is complete, they are clearly only of use at this time of the year.

▽ *The oranda has a raspberrylike growth called a hood on its head.*

HOODED GOLDFISH

Goldfish that have raspberrylike growths on their heads (above) are referred to as hooded varieties. Goldfish enthusiasts place great value on the size and position of the hood. If it is only on the top of the head, it is known as "cranial." If it is located under the eyes, it is known as "infraorbital." If the hood is on the cheeks, it is known as "opercular."

The relative sizes of these three features determine the quality of the goldfish and are the subject of heated debate among experts. There are even some goldfish fans who dedicate themselves exclusively to the care, breeding, and appreciation of just a single variety of hooded goldfish.

GOURAMIS

It seems unbelievable that a fish can drown. Yet this is precisely what happens in some species, such as gouramis, if they are prevented from surfacing regularly to take in a gulp of air.

ADVANCED BONY FISH

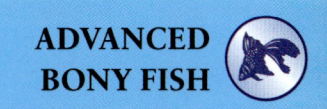

Gouramis have evolved to live in waters that can become very low in oxygen. Under such conditions, most fish would sooner or later choke to death. In gouramis, however, some of the gills have developed into special organs that are very efficient at absorbing oxygen directly from the air.

The Price of Survival

This survival strategy comes at a price, though, since the highly modified gills can no longer absorb oxygen from the water. Therefore, even if there is an ample supply of dissolved oxygen in the water, gouramis cannot obtain as much as they need through their gills. They must regularly come to the surface to breathe. If they cannot do this, they will die.

Many species also use air to blow mucus-covered bubbles. During the breeding season the males of these species build bubble nests on the surface, or under a submerged leaf. Eggs are laid in these bubbles and develop in an oxygen-rich environment. In other species, males carry the eggs in their mouths until they are ready to hatch. Since these males must come to the surface for air, the eggs also receive plenty of oxygen, even if there is little dissolved oxygen in the water.

In the breeding season, males become very aggressive. In some species of fighting fish this aggression lasts all year. In the Far East, fish-fighting contests between these fish are held, with bets placed on the outcome.

A pair of Siamese fighting fish (male on the left) mating beneath their floating bubble nest. The eggs are placed in the nest and guarded by the male.

Fact File

GOURAMIS

Families: Helostomatidae, Osphronemidae, Belontiidae (about 90 species altogether)

Order: Perciformes

Where do they live?: Widely distributed in Southeast Asia, India, Pakistan, Thailand, and the Malay Archipelago

Habitat: Wide range of still or slow-flowing waters, often with overhanging and submerged vegetation; some of these waters may become depleted of oxygen

Size: From about 1 inch (2.5 cm), as in some croaking gourami species, to over 30 inches (76 cm) in the giant gouramis

Coloration: Vary variable and usually more pronounced in males, especially during the breeding season

Diet: Plants and small animals (mostly invertebrates)

Breeding: Bubble-nesting species build foam rafts on the water surface or under an overhang or submerged leaf; mouthbrooding species carry the eggs in the mouth; eggs usually hatch within a day or two

Status: 3 species of fighting fish are critically endangered; the jealous fighting fish and one species of the liquorice gouramis are endangered; 7 other *Betta* species are vulnerable

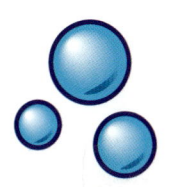

GRAY WHALE

Gray whales are long-distance travelers, feeding in the far north and breeding in the tropics. Every year gray whales migrate more than 12,000 miles. Because they nearly always travel in sight of land, these whales are easy to watch.

SEA MAMMALS

Gray whales are a fairly common sight along the west coast of North America. In spring and fall, thousands of people travel there every year to see gray whales pass by on their long migrations. However, fifty years ago, these huge mammals were almost extinct. They had been hunted for hundreds of years for meat and oil. The gray whale population had fallen to just a few thousand individuals. Today they are protected, and the only people allowed to hunt gray whales are Inuits and Native Americans, who use traditional methods and kill only a few whales each year. There are now around 25,000 gray whales living in the eastern Pacific Ocean.

Gray whales have a distinctive shape. Instead of a dorsal (back) fin, they have a row of bumps running along the lower part of the back. In adults, the skin is always blotchy and covered with big clumps of barnacles.

Winter Feeding, Summer Breeding

Female gray whales are pregnant for thirteen months and rear only one calf every other year. They mate one winter, give birth during the next winter, and mate again during the third winter. Newborn gray whales are much skinnier than adults. It takes the calf a few months to build up a thick enough layer of blubber, or fat, to cope with living in cold water, so the mother must travel somewhere warm to give birth. That is why gray whales travel south to gather every winter in the warm, shallow waters of Baja California, off the coast of Mexico.

A big, barnacled gray whale breaches. A breach is when a whale leaps halfway or more out of the water and then falls back onto its side.

Fact File

GRAY WHALE

Eschrichtius robustus
Family: Eschrichtidae
Order: Cetacea

Where do they live?: Coastal areas of Pacific Ocean, from Baja California and Japan to Arctic waters

Habitat: Coastal waters less than 330 feet (100 m) deep

Size: Head–body length 39–50 feet (12–15 m); weight 18–38 tons (16–34 metric tons)

Skin: Mottled gray, with patches of barnacles and whale lice

Diet: Plankton and bottom-living invertebrates, mostly small crustaceans

Breeding: Single calf born after 13 months' inside mother's body; weaned at 7 months; able to breed at around 8 years

Life span: Up to 77 years

Status: No longer hunted intensively, but conservation measures needed to protect it; the population around Japan is critically endangered

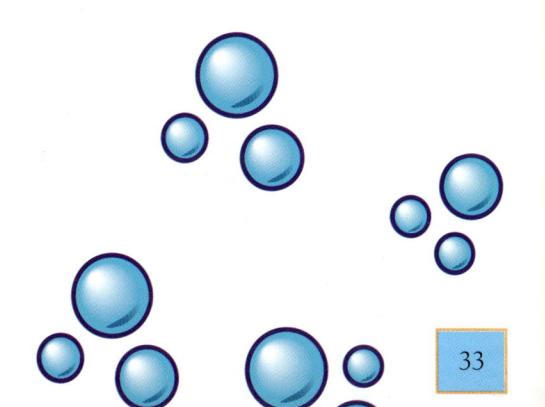

GRAY WHALE

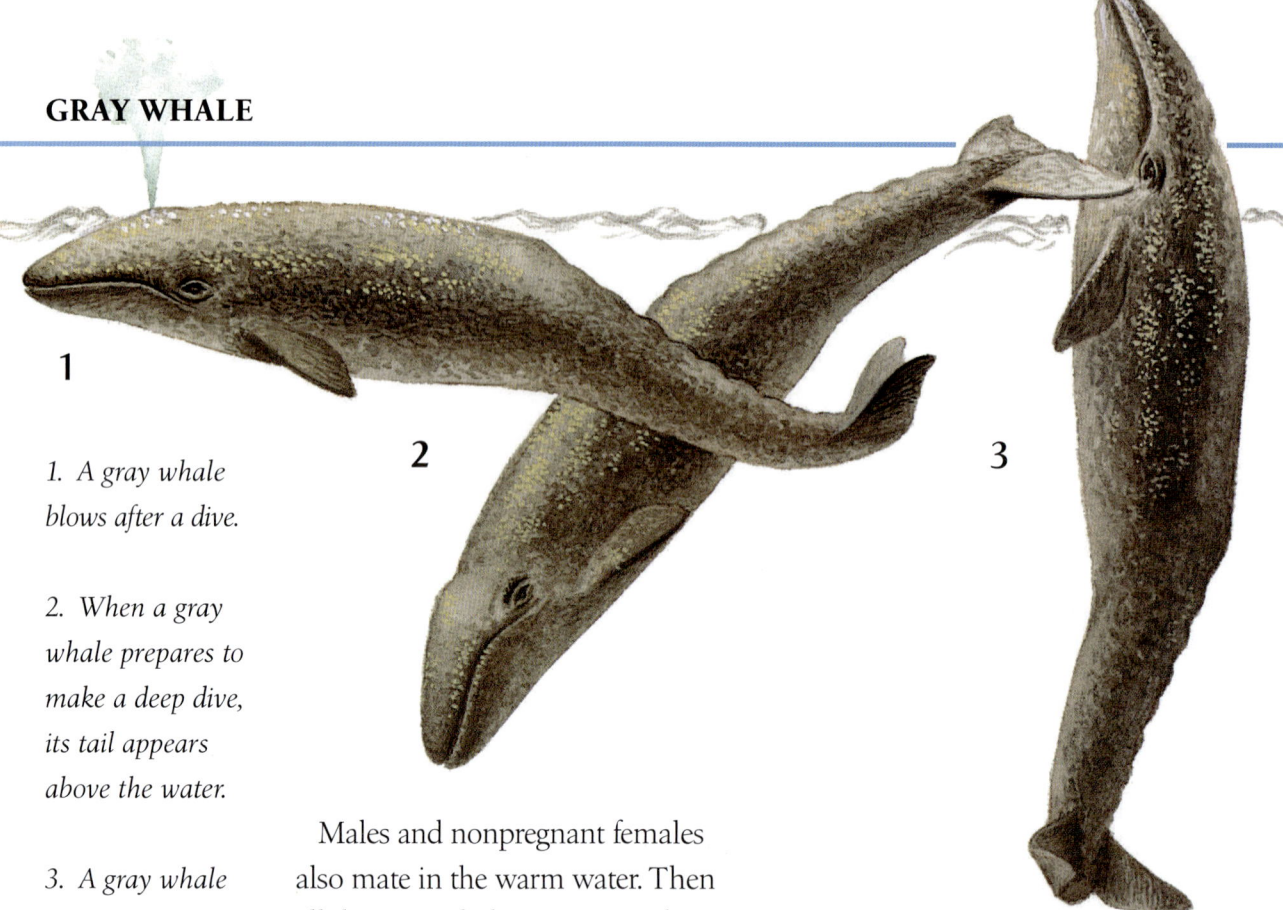

1. A gray whale blows after a dive.

2. When a gray whale prepares to make a deep dive, its tail appears above the water.

3. A gray whale "spy-hops," sticking its head above the water to check its surroundings.

4. A gray whale mother swims with her calf.

Males and nonpregnant females also mate in the warm water. Then all the gray whales return north to cold waters in the spring.

Gray whale calves grow amazingly fast—the mother's milk is extremely fattening and a calf can gain up to 70 pounds a day. By the time the calves reach Arctic waters, at around six or seven months old, they are fat enough to survive the cold and ready to begin eating solid food.

Gray whales eat mainly small, flealike crustaceans called amphipods. In midsummer, billions of these creatures are present. The long hours of daylight encourage the algae and other plankton (microscopic animals and plantlike life-forms) on which amphipods feed to grow and reproduce superfast.

Sieve Eaters

Amphipods live in the seabed, and gray whales have an unusual way of feeding. The whales swim to the seafloor and plow along

SEA MAMMALS

Gray whales often swim within half a mile of shore, which makes them easy to watch closely.

the bottom with their mouth open. They take in lots of mud and sand, along with the amphipods and other small buried animals. Instead of teeth, gray whales have a mouth full of bristly combs, called baleen. Baleen acts as a sieve to collect the food, while the mud and sand pass through the baleen with the water and leave the mouth. From above, feeding gray whales are easy to spot because they create clouds of stirred-up mud from the ocean floor and leave long furrows in the seabed.

Having fed well all summer, adult whales return to Baja California in the fall. Males and females whose calves have just weaned go there to mate. Once the females are pregnant, the gray whales quickly travel north to begin feeding again.

DID YOU KNOW?
- Most gray whales turn on their right side to feed on the seabed.
- A gray whale that lives to be seventy years old will have swum approximately 750,000 miles on migrations!
- A large gray whale may have up to 350 pounds of barnacles attached to its body!

WHALE WATCHING

Gray whales are curious animals. They often swim toward boats and seem interested in people. Some gray whales come right alongside small boats and even allow themselves to be stroked. Being so trusting and inquisitive once made gray whales easy targets for hunters. Now gray whales are protected, and the boats that go out in search of them are full of whale watchers instead of hunters.

Hunted by Killer Whales

Apart from humans, the only other animals that hunt gray whales are killer whales, or orcas. Orcas hunt in groups and target young calves. The gray whale mother can do very little to protect her calf once orcas begin an attack. Gray whale calves cannot swim fast enough to get away, but sometimes they can hide from orcas in dense patches of seaweed.

GREAT WHITE SHARK

It is many people's worst nightmare. Yet, for all its awesome reputation, the superbly adapted great white shark has more to fear from humans than we have to fear from it.

CARTILAGINOUS FISH

The great white is the perfect hunting machine. It can detect prey from distances of over a mile. Then it homes in, using a battery of senses. These include the ability to detect electric impulses given off by the prey as well as chemical signals such as minute traces of blood. Its sight is also very keen, especially in clear water. The shark's streamlined, torpedo-shaped body and powerful tail allow it to put on impressive bursts of speed so it can quickly approach any selected victim. It also has massive jaws and fearsome teeth that can inflict fatal injuries in a split second.

Declining Numbers

While the great white shark is not primarily hunted for food, its numbers are declining worldwide. Sport fishing accounts for many deaths, but these top predators are also taken because their jaws and teeth are much sought after as curios. Nets set out along shark-threatened coastlines to protect bathers drown many of these sharks, as do nets and lines set out to catch other species.

Great whites take between ten and twelve years to mature. Since they produce very few young in each brood, this also creates further pressure on wild populations of the species. Some estimates put the total remaining number of these sharks at around 10,000. Since the 1990s there have been protection programs in place in an attempt to save this awe-inspiring fish.

Attacks on humans by great whites are actually very rare. Only a few of the fifty or so officially recorded shark attacks every year are attributed to this species.

Fact File

GREAT WHITE SHARK

Carcharodon carcharias
Family: Lamnidae
Order: Lamniformes

Where do they live?: Mainly warm-temperate and subtropical waters, but also found in warmer areas

Habitat: Wide range of habitats from the surf line to offshore (but rarely in mid ocean), and from surface waters down to depths exceeding 820 feet (250 m)—although it has also been reported from a depth of over 4,000 feet (over 1,200 m)

Size: Specimens in excess of 36 feet (11 m) have been reported, but confirmed data indicate a size of 18–20 feet (5.5–6 m)

Coloration: Top half of the body is slate gray to brownish; irregular line separates the top half from the pure white lower half of the body; the underside of the pectoral (chest) fins has blackish tips

Diet: Mainly fish—including other sharks—as well as turtles, seabirds, seals, sea lions, and dolphins

Breeding: Eggs are fertilized inside the body of the female and take up to a year to develop; female gives birth to 5–14 young which can measure 5 feet (1.5 m) at birth

Status: Listed as vulnerable

GRUNION

On some Californian beaches there is a spectacle like no other during nights of a full moon. Millions of fish launch themselves ashore in an apparent mass suicide attempt.

ADVANCED BONY FISH

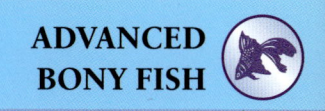

Although for a fish to launch itself onto a beach may seem like a life-threatening action, it is in fact simply a spawning technique. It is used by one or two fish species, including the grunion and the capelin. Many of these fish die during these dangerous onshore excursions, but it is all in the cause of breeding.

The goal is for egg- and sperm-laden fish to be swept far up shore by the waves and to be left stranded there for a few seconds. During this brief period, females bury the back half of their bodies into the soft wet sand, positioning themselves in an upright position. As this happens, a number of males surround each female. The female then releases her eggs under the sand, and the males release their sperm, thus fertilizing the eggs. With luck, the next large wave will sweep the females and males back into the safety of the surf.

Spring Tide Hatching

Spawning happens during the full moon when tides are at their highest. The eggs will remain buried in the sand above water level for the next two weeks, until the highest tides are due again. During this time, the embryos develop inside the eggs. They hatch within minutes of being wetted by the first waves of the incoming high tide and are washed into the sea.

It takes the young fish one year to mature. They then return to the beaches to breed and take part in the same dangerous life-and-death ritual.

Grunions spawn on a beach at night. This is a dangerous activity for a fish; many of them never make it back to the sea but fall victim to predators.

Fact File

GRUNION

Leuresthes tenuis

Subfamily: Atherinopsinae
Family: Atherinidae
Order: Atheriniformes

Where do they live?: West coast of North America, from southern California to Baja California

Habitat: Mainly found in shallow inshore seas, usually at or near the surface

Size: Up to 7.5 inches (19 cm)

Coloration: Dark blue along the back, with silvery sides and belly

Diet: Mainly small invertebrates

Breeding: Eggs buried about 3 inches (8 cm) under the sand along the spring tide strandline and abandoned; hatching takes 2 weeks

Status: Not known to be threatened

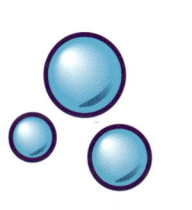

GUPPY

Also once known as the "millions fish," because of the large numbers in which it was found in the wild, the guppy has been thrilling fishkeepers for around a hundred years.

ADVANCED BONY FISH

This species was originally named the millions fish, but the name guppy is used mainly today. This is in honor of the Reverend Lechmere Guppy who discovered this fish in Trinidad in the 1860s—even though it had in fact been described a few years earlier by the German naturalist Wilhelm Peters.

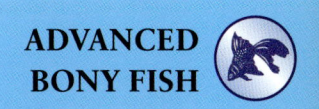

Tiny Beauties

Wild male guppies are about an inch long. However, they pack much beauty into their tiny bodies, and have been hot favorites with fishkeepers for nearly as long as the hobby of fishkeeping has been in existence. Few fish can compete with male guppies in terms of the richness of color and fin variations seen in specimens bred by fishkeepers. The range of varieties that exists is bewildering, and more are created every year.

In a sense, guppy breeding is similar to goldfish breeding, because any combination of colors can be found with any of the various caudal (tail) fin shapes. Since wild populations are highly variable anyway, the scope for new combinations is infinite.

Today's guppies have larger bodies than their wild ancestors. The tail of the vast majority of modern-day varieties is also many times longer and broader; so is the dorsal (back) fin. The females have colorful bodies, which are in sharp contrast to the drab, uniform body color of wild females. These changes have come about through careful breeding by fishkeepers.

The guppy is bred in many different fin shapes and body colors. Any fin characteristic can be combined with any color, so the scope for new varieties is huge.

Fact File

GUPPY

Poecilia reticulata
Family: Poeciliidae
Order: Cyprinodontiformes

Where do they live?: Originally found north of the Amazon River in South America (in Venezuela and parts of northern Brazil) as well as the West Indies; it has also been introduced into many U.S. states—including Florida—as well as to parts of Africa and Asia

Habitat: Wide range of shallow freshwater habitats, including forest streams, lakes, and ditches

Size: Males around 1 inch (2.5 cm); females about twice this size; cultivated varieties are larger

Coloration: Extremely variable in males, which have numerous dots, patches, and streaks of different colors; wild females quite drab; in bred varieties, many females are also colored

Diet: Mostly small invertebrates and plant matter

Breeding: Eggs are fertilized inside the female and take 4–6 weeks to develop; broods can number nearly 200 but are usually much smaller than this

Status: Not known to be threatened

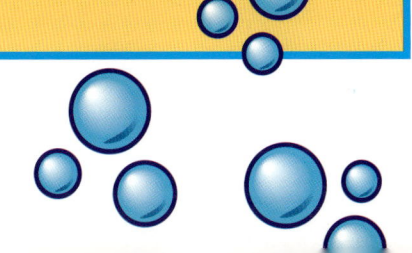

41

GUPPY

Worldwide Species

The guppy is a native of the Amazon River of South America and also of parts of the West Indies such as Trinidad and Barbados.

However, it has been introduced into many other countries over the years. One of the aims of these introductions has been to control the mosquitoes that carry malaria. Although guppies do not eat the adult mosquitoes, they eat large amounts of their aquatic larvae if given the chance. The species has also been introduced into all the countries and regions where fish are bred for home aquariums.

▼ *This guppy has a delta tail. Tail shapes in guppies include ones that look like flags and spades. Other guppy tails have long, pointed extensions.*

DID YOU KNOW?

- Baby guppies do not gain weight during development and are born weighing the same as, or less than, a fertilized egg.
- Female guppies can store sperm and can use these to fertilize a number of egg batches over a period of time.
- Guppies were first bred in captivity in 1908.

Back to Nature

Sometimes, guppies have escaped from breeding establishments into ditches and other waterways. Over many generations they have lost their large flowing tails and dorsal fins and have gradually become very much like their wild ancestors, with small bodies and short tails.

This happens because large-finned individuals cannot swim as fast as short-finned ones. Predators pick them off, while short-finned specimens escape. As a result, short-finned individuals soon outnumber their long-finned relatives. Eventually, these populations end up consisting just of guppies which are short-finned, well-adapted, fast swimmers.

Mother Care

Guppies belong to a large subfamily of fish that differ from many others because they do not lay eggs. Instead, they give birth to fully formed babies. In these fish, called livebearers, the eggs are fertilized inside the body of the females. Once fertilized, they are kept inside the female's body while they develop. They hatch there and the babies are released by the mother.

This way of breeding gives developing embryos a high degree of protection, since the female carries them with her wherever she goes. As long as the mother survives and does not fall victim to a predator, all her young stay safe until they are born. Once born, however, they are left to survive on their own.

▽ 1. A wild guppy male
2. A double sword male
3. A deltatail male
4. A long dorsal veiltail male

REMARKABLE BELLY FIN

Male guppies have a specially modified belly (anal) fin that looks like a rod. This "rod" consists of fin rays which lie one behind the other as in normal anal fins. However, each ray is highly modified, bearing hooks, blades, or claws.

This unusually structured anal fin—known as a gonopodium—is used by a male to introduce sperm into the body of the female during mating. As the gonopodium is swung forward to make contact with the female's belly opening (known as the vent), the rays fold over each other. They form a temporary groove or channel along which the sperm travel into the female's vent.

HAGFISH AND LAMPREYS

Hagfish and lampreys have no jaws, so they cannot bite like other fish. However, this has not stopped them being the only surviving species of an otherwise extinct group of primitive fish.

PRIMITIVE FISH

Fish first evolved in the Cambrian seas, between 400 and 500 million years ago. They were very different from the ones we know today. For example, some were armored and had a stiffening rod made of cartilage along their bodies, instead of a backbone. Two groups of these primitive fish, the hagfish and the lampreys, still exist today.

Hagfish and the lampreys have features in common, but they are not closely related. Neither of them have jaws, backbones, or paired fins, but they have paired eyes and a primitive third eye on top of the head. Unlike their ancient relatives, however, their eel-like bodies are not armored. Hagfish have a paddlelike tail and lampreys have one or two dorsal (back) fins.

Feasting and Fasting

Adult hagfish and lampreys prey on other animals. Hagfish scavenge on the flesh of dying or dead fish, dolphins, and whales. They can locate their food from great distances using their well-developed senses. They make a hole in the side of their victim's body, using a specialized biting tongue and rasping plates around the mouth. Hundreds of hagfish may feed on a whale carcass lying on the seabed. By burying their heads inside the carcass they can consume all of its flesh, leaving a bag of skin and bone! Adult lampreys can be parasites of live fish, feeding rather like hagfish by grasping the host with their suckerlike mouth and

The suckerlike mouth disk can be seen in this brook lamprey. The holes behind the eye are gill openings. Brook lampreys grow to a length of about 6 inches.

Fact File

HAGFISH AND LAMPREYS

Orders: Myxiniformes (hagfish; about 50 species), Petromyzontiformes (lampreys; about 40 species)

Class: Cyclostomata

Superclass: Agnatha

Where do they live?: Hagfish: worldwide in all oceans; lampreys: worldwide in all oceans, and in rivers and lakes

Habitat: Hagfish: seabeds below 72°F (22° C), often burrowing in mud; lampreys: midwater and on beds of seas, lakes, and rivers

Size: Hagfish up to 46 inches (1.2 m) long; lampreys up to 36 inches (92 cm) long

Coloration: Hagfish: depends on species—white, pink, blue-gray, or black; lampreys: larvae pale and transparent; adults orange, brown, gray, or black, paler below

Diet: Hagfish: carrion feeders or scavengers; lamprey larvae feed on organic particles; adults non-feeding or parasitic on other fish

Breeding: Hagfish and lampreys release sperm and eggs into water where fertilization occurs; a more complex life cycle with a swimming larva occurs in lampreys

Status: Hagfish: unknown; lampreys: in most cases not known, but some brook lampreys are rare or vulnerable

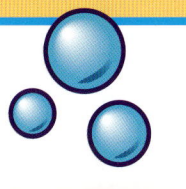

HAGFISH AND LAMPREYS

◗ *This hagfish eating its way inside a dead fish has formed its body into a knot to gain extra leverage.*

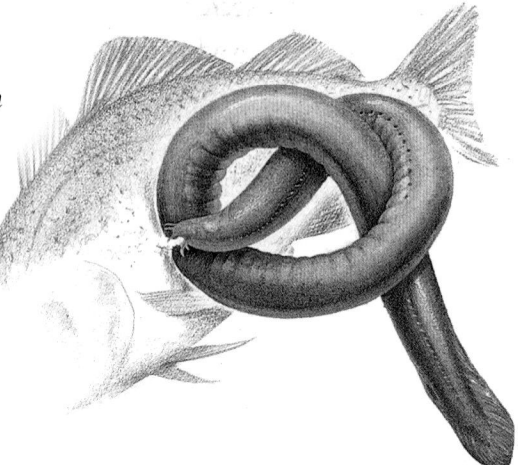

▼ *A hagfish's central mouth is surrounded by sensory tentacles. The animal has no true eyes.*

opening a wound with the rasping tongue before eating its flesh and blood. Brook, or dwarf, lampreys do not feed at all when they reach adulthood. Instead, they rely on food reserves stored in their bodies when they are larvae.

Lamprey Life Cycles

Hagfish live in the sea, laying a small number of eggs during spawning. They do not die afterwards.

Lampreys spawn in fresh water, so marine species must migrate, often 600 miles or more, to reach their breeding grounds. They swim in an eel-like fashion using their single dorsal (back) fin. Whether or not they return to the same river is not known. They get used to fresh water in the estuary before moving up river.

When the lampreys have found a suitable gravel bed, they dig out a shallow area to form a nest. They spawn in pairs, the female anchoring her body by sucking on a large pebble while the male attaches himself to her. Eggs and sperm are released and fertilization occurs in the water. The animals then writhe their bodies about to cover the fertilized eggs with gravel.

Lampreys that live in fresh water also migrate—for example, from lakes into streams. Brook lampreys spawn in groups over a shared nest. Once spawning is over, lampreys die.

Going to Sea

After two or three weeks the eggs hatch into larvae. They resemble minute, transparent lampreys, being colorless at night and dark by day. Their mouth is covered by a funnel-like hood bearing tentacles. These

PRIMITIVE FISH

DID YOU KNOW?

- Hagfish have four main hearts and two pairs of smaller secondary ones. Lampreys have one heart.

- Hagfish have five to fourteen pairs of gill openings. Lampreys have seven pairs of gill openings.

- Young hagfish hatch out as hermaphrodites (having male and female sex organs), but they lose one reproductive organ as they mature and become single sexed.

small animals are swept downstream by the current until they reach slower-flowing water. Then they burrow in the silt. They feed by filtering organic particles from the water, trapping them with their tentacles and a slimy secretion. As they grow they develop adult features and become yellowish brown in color. Then they are ready to go to sea and begin their parasitic lives.

Eating Lampreys

Lampreys have been thought of as a delicacy for centuries. King Henry I of England died of a "surfeit of lampreys" in 1135, but today there is no largescale commercial industry based around using lampreys for food. However, lampreys can be serious pests in fish farms where great numbers can ruin the fish stocks. Even in open sea fisheries they can cause damage to the catch.

▼ *Lamprey eyes are quite large compared with the tiny eyes of hagfish.*

LIGHT AND VISION IN LAMPREYS

The eyes on either side of the head of lampreys resemble the eyes of other fish. Lampreys are active in the daytime and are thought to use both sight and smell to find their prey. Their third eye is situated on top, but not quite in the middle, of the head, and is formed from part of the brain. Along with light receptors in the skin in other parts of the body, it responds to changes in light intensity. In the larvae, whose paired eyes are covered with skin, this third eye may be important for controlling the color changes that the animals make. The eyes of hagfish are small, very basic structures.

HAMMERHEAD SHARKS

When viewed from the side, it looks very much like any other shark. However, when seen head-on, or from above or below, a hammerhead is one of the most unusual sharks you could imagine.

CARTILAGINOUS FISH

Other sharks have pointed or rounded snouts, but hammerheads live up to their name. Their unusual hammerlike heads make them the most easily identifiable of all the sharks. Although the head of these sharks is often described as being the shape of a hammer, it is, in fact, more like a "T" with a curved top.

Useful Hammer

In cross-section, the hammer is shaped like a wing. It may also act like a wing, giving some lift to these sharks. They spend a great deal of time hunting near the bottom, and their fins are well adapted for this way of life. But when they swim in open water, the winglike hammer may help them. Also, by having the nostrils and other senses on the tips of the hammer, the shark may more easily find its prey. The broadly spaced eyes cover a wider field of vision.

It is reported that the great hammerhead uses its hammer to head-butt skates and rays (two species of fish hunted by hammerheads) and pin them to the bottom. Having immobilized the prey, the shark spins round and bites pieces off the victim's winglike fins, preventing it from escaping.

Sometimes scalloped hammerhead sharks gather in huge schools (called shivers) numbering over 200 individuals. No hunting is involved when this happens, however. It is more likely that mating, rather than eating, is the reason for these mass get-togethers.

This scalloped hammerhead shark is swimming near the Galapagos Islands. Its "hammer" has a series of indentations or scallops, giving it its common name.

Fact File

HAMMERHEAD SHARKS

Family: Sphyrnidae (8 or 9 species)
Order: Carcharhiniformes

Where do they live?: Widespread in many tropical and warm-temperate regions

Habitat: Open and shallow waters, ranging from inshore reefs to around 1,000 feet (300 m) in the scalloped hammerhead; most species remain in the upper 260 feet (80 m); many species also hunt along the bottom

Size: From around 36 inches (92 cm) in the scalloped bonnethead to around 19.7 feet (6 m) in the great hammerhead

Coloration: Grayish-blue along the back, fading to a light-colored belly

Diet: Wide range of prey, from fish (including other sharks), to squid, crustaceans, and sea snakes

Breeding: Eggs are fertilized inside the mother's body and take around 8 months to develop; female gives birth to 6–40 young (known as pups), depending on size and species

Status: Great hammerhead is listed as endangered; concern also surrounds most of the other species because of uncontrolled overfishing

HATCHETFISH

Hatchetfish are the freshwater counterparts of the sea-dwelling flying fish. However, hatchetfish go a significant step further; they can genuinely fly, instead of simply gliding above the water.

ADVANCED BONY FISH

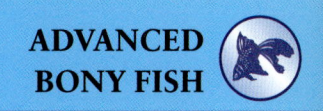

Freshwater hatchetfish are sometimes called flying characins—a direct reference to the technique they use to escape predators. When threatened, they shoot out of the water and, quite literally, disappear. This usually confuses a predator sufficiently to allow the hatchetfish to escape.

Perfect Flying Equipment

Various body modifications make this remarkable ability possible. The chest, for instance, is very deep and hatchetlike—hence the common name for the fish. It has powerful muscles that can provide the thrust needed to propel the fish clear of the water. In addition, the chest is very narrow, and it forms a keel (a deep V-shape, like the bottom of a boat) that can cut through the water with very little resistance.

The pectoral (chest) fins are long and slim and have a strong, slightly curved front edge, almost like wings. The fins are high up on the body, just behind the head. The back, from the snout to the dorsal (back) fin, is straight. This shape makes it easier for the hatchetfish to swim near the water's surface.

As well as all these characteristics, the fish has a powerful tail. The combination of all these features means that a hatchetfish can jump out of the water and then fly by flapping its strong pectoral fins. When chased, hatchetfish can fly for a short distance at a height of 4 inches above the water surface.

The mouth of a hatchetfish (these are common hatchetfish) is turned upward. This helps the fish snatch insects from the surface as it feeds.

Fact File

HATCHETFISH

Family: Gasteropelecidae (9 species)
Order: Characiformes

Where do they live?: Panama and all South American countries except Chile

Habitat: Some species, such as the marbled hatchetfish, live in small streams and creeks; others, such as the spotted hatchetfish and the giant hatchetfish, live in more open waters

Size: From 1 inch (2.5 cm) to around 3 inches (8 cm)

Coloration: All species have silvery scales on the sides and belly; several species have dark central body lines extending as far as the tail

Diet: Mostly insects but also aquatic invertebrates

Breeding: Eggs are scattered among the roots of floating plants and among fine-leaved vegetation and abandoned; hatching takes about 1.5 days

Status: Not known to be threatened

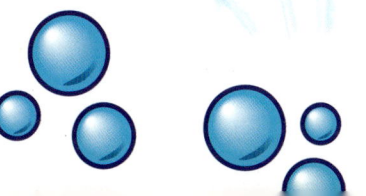

HERMIT CRABS

Instead of growing a natural shell of its own, the hermit crab makes use of a secondhand shell for protection. It often shares this "home" with other animals such as sea anemones, barnacles, and worms.

INVERTEBRATES

Hermit crabs are scavengers on the seashore and seabed. They differ from the true crabs because they do not have a fifth pair of walking legs. Their fourth pair of legs is very small and can be seen only when the animal is removed from its snail shell home. This pair of legs grips the inside of the shell and holds the animal in place. The abdomen is not folded under the front of the body as it is in the true crabs. Instead it is long and twisted to the right so that it fits into the snail shell easily. The abdomen is also soft, so the protection given by the snail shell is very important.

When disturbed, the hermit crab retreats into its shell, but when it feels safe it emerges partially and the first three pairs of walking legs can be seen. The first pair has large nippers; the nipper on one leg is bigger than the nipper on the other. The nippers fit neatly into the opening of the shell and close it off when the crab is completely inside. The second and third pairs of legs have claws at the tips for walking.

Moving Home

A hermit crab outside its snail shell is vulnerable to predators, so moving house is a dangerous time. A growing hermit soon finds its shell is too small and goes in search of a new one, which it finds simply by looking. Having carefully checked out the new shell, it must move in quickly before another hermit grabs the shell or a predator spots the crab.

Hermit crabs often fight over ownership of shells. A large shell helps to make the crab appear bigger, too, helping it frighten off other crabs.

Fact File

HERMIT CRABS

Infraorder: Anomura (several hundred species altogether)

Order: Decapoda

Class: Malacostraca

Subphylum: Crustacea

Phylum: Arthropoda

Where do they live?: Worldwide in all seas and oceans

Habitat: Seashore and seabed

Size: Rarely longer that 6 inches (15 cm); a few relatives that lack shells may reach 12 inches (30 cm)

Coloration: The crab itself may be a variety of colors, from yellowish brown to dark red; some tropical species are brightly patterned; some are very hairy

Diet: Almost anything edible they can find; a few species filter water to get food particles

Breeding: Sexual reproduction: mating must take place when the crabs are out of their shells; the fertilized eggs adhere to the females' abdomen inside the shell until the larvae hatch out; these develop through several phases until the adult stage is developed

Status: Not known

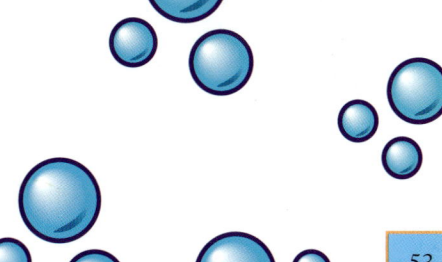

HERRING

They are 140 million years old, perhaps even older.
Yet, within a few human generations, we have
managed to bring herring, pilchards, and sardines
to the brink of extinction.

ADVANCED BONY FISH

Herring, and their close relatives such as pilchards and anchovies, have long been extremely important to humankind. They have been responsible for the rise and fall of nations, making fortunes for some while ruining others. Countries have even gone to war in an effort to secure stocks of these valuable fish. Britain and Holland, for example, fought a bloody war in the late 1600s over fishing rights.

A most unusual battle was also fought in 1429 between the French and Scots on one side, and the English on the other. It began when a wagon train was attacked while transporting salted herring to English troops who were laying siege to the city of Orleans. The fish were on their way to the troops so that they could observe the strict religious rules of the day, which dictated that fish be eaten during Lent. Although the English won the Battle of the Herring, the wagonload of fish ended up being scattered all over the battlefield.

Feast and Famine

There have been times when stocks of herring, pilchards, and sardines have been so abundant that they have appeared limitless. At other times, stocks have disappeared and, with them, have gone wealth and a vitally important food resource.

An indication of the importance of these fish can be gained from the fact that, in the 1930s, herring and

In the Sea of Cortez, a brown pelican dives for herring. These fish, and similar species such as anchovies, are a vital part of the marine food chain.

Fact File

HERRING

Family: Clupeidae (about 180 species)

Order: Clupeiformes

Where do they live?: Oceans, seas, and coastal areas worldwide; some species live in fresh water

Habitat: Found in shallow waters or close to the surface; some species spend time in estuaries; others are found permanently in rivers and lakes

Size: Most under 20 inches (50 cm) long; "sardines" usually 4–6 inches (10–15 cm); pilchards 10 inches (25 cm); herring up to 18 inches (46 cm); largest species, the giant freshwater herring, 5 feet (1.5 m)

Coloration: Most species dark-gray or brownish-gray on back, with or without dark spots; sides and belly silvery

Diet: Almost exclusively plankton; fish larvae also eaten by some species

Breeding: Spawning in large schools; pilchards produce glassy floating eggs that hatch in 2–4 days; herring produce sticky sinking eggs that hatch after 8–9 days in warm water, or 6–7 weeks if the water is cold

Status: One member of the family, *Alosa vistonica*, is critically endangered; the Alabama shad and *Tenualosa thibaudeaui* are endangered; the Macedonian shad and the Venezuelan herring are vulnerable

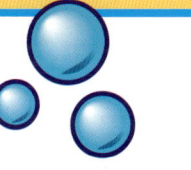

HERRING

◐ Pilchards are a plentiful and cheap source of food for people in many parts of the world.

their closest relatives such as sardines accounted for one third of all the fish caught in the world. Even in the late decades of the last century, as many as 3,300 million tons of Atlantic herring were caught each year.

In the end, stocks were brought to the point of collapse. Today, though, there are fishing quotas that determine how many tons of these fish can be harvested. As a result, stocks are showing signs of recovery in some of the main fishing areas.

Healthy "Brain Food"

Herring, pilchards, sardines, and several other close relatives all look very similar. Most are dark blue along the back and silvery along the sides and belly. Their scales are sometimes said to be "deciduous,"

HERRING LIE ABOUT THEIR AGE

As they grow, herring (below) lay down rings in their scales, in the way that a tree produces annual growth rings. So by counting the rings, it is possible for scientists to figure out the age of the fish. However, many of the scales on an individual may be younger than the fish itself. It is therefore often difficult to tell the exact age of a herring without counting all the scales and using the oldest one as a guide—always assuming, of course, that this scale is one of the original ones the fish was born with and not a replacement scale.

ADVANCED BONY FISH

DID YOU KNOW?

- Humpback whales hunt herring by blowing a net of bubbles around them. This drives the fish into a tight ball that can be easily swallowed by the whales.
- Nets set out for herring, pilchards, and sardines sometimes trap other victims, such as dolphins, that can drown as a result.
- About forty-four species of West African herring spend their entire lives in fresh water.

which means that they drop off easily (as leaves drop from deciduous trees in the fall).

The common names are also used quite loosely, so it is often difficult to tell which species is being described. In many countries, for example, a sardine is just a small pilchard. In others, the word sardine refers to a particular species. Most of these are, however, considerably smaller when fully grown than a herring, which grows to about 18 inches in length.

All species are tasty fish that contain a rich supply of Omega 3 oils. These are thought by many people to be good for human health, especially the heart. Because of these sorts of oils, herring, pilchards, and sardines are called "brain food."

School Protection

All the members of the herring family are schooling fish. In other words, they live in large groups or shoals. Often the schools consist of many thousands of fish. They can grow to countless millions during the migrations by these fish when on their way to new feeding grounds or to breed.

When schools are attacked, they form a tight ball, known as a "bait ball." The whirling bodies of fish can confuse attackers. Even if a "ball" does not have this effect, each fish benefits by being less likely to be eaten than if it were on its own, or among just a few other fish.

Young farmed herring in a pen—part of the Fish Enhancement Program in British Columbia, Canada. When released, they will help restore wild stock levels.

57

HYDROZOANS

Hydrozoans include a wide range of sedentary and swimming marine and freshwater animals. They are relatives of the sea anemones, corals, and jellyfish and have complex life cycles.

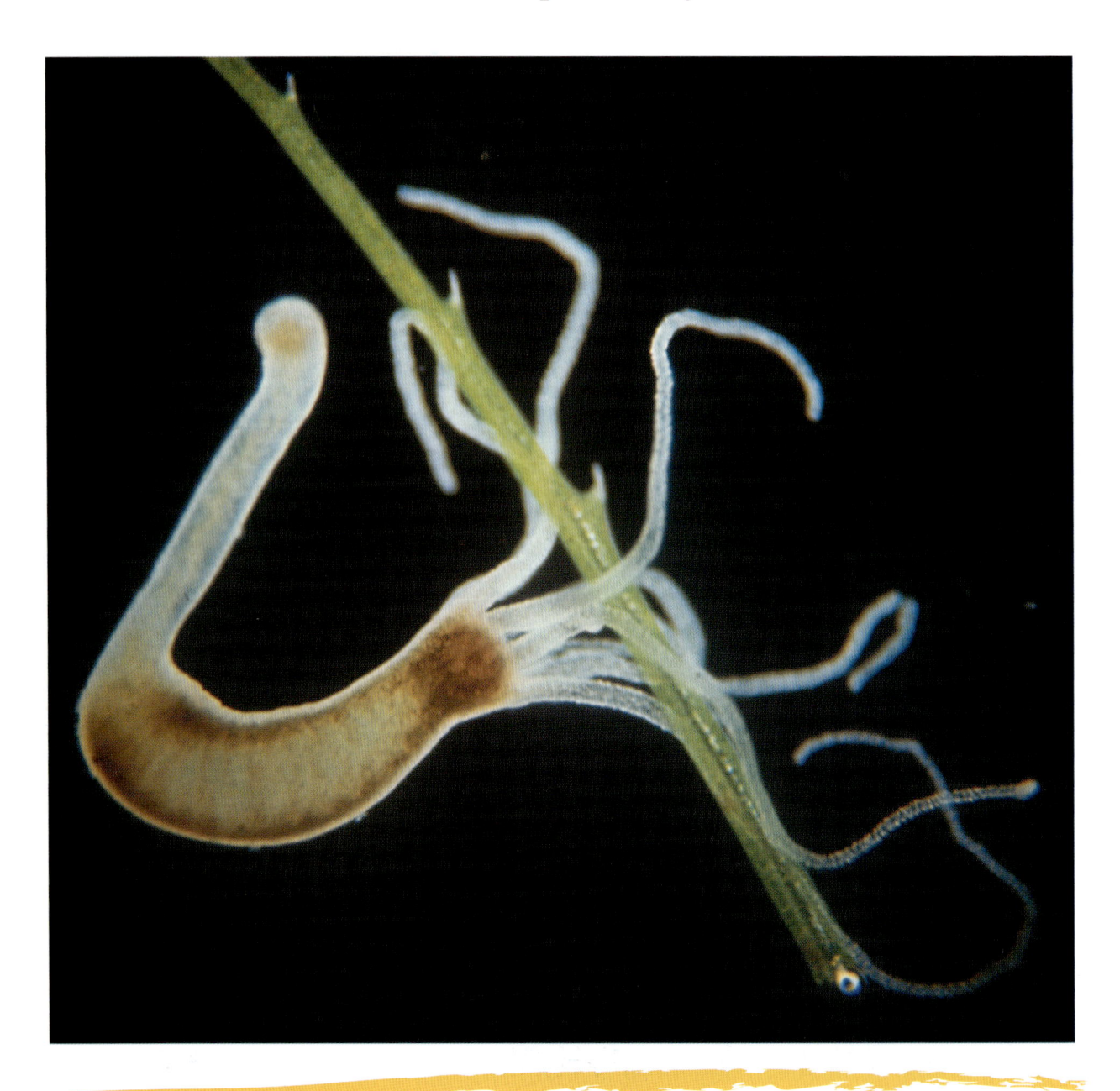

INVERTEBRATES

Each animal is known as a polyp, and it may live singly or as one individual in a colony with other polyps. Each polyp has a simple, saclike body with a mouth but no anus. This mouth is surrounded by stinging tentacles that are used to catch prey and for defense. The shape and style of the polyps vary between the different groups.

Hydroids form a large group within the hydrozoans. They may be solitary or colonial. A colony consists of many feeding polyps plus a few reproductive polyps. The hydrocorals are tropical hydrozoans with stony skeletons that resemble reef-building corals. They have powerful stinging cells, so they are called fire corals.

Complex Life Cycle

The life cycle of almost all hydrozoans starts when a bottom-dwelling colony produces a jellyfishlike stage called a medusa. Each medusa drifts in the plankton and develops male and female organs. In turn sperms and eggs are released into the sea and a small larva forms. This ultimately settles back on the seabed to form a new bottom-dwelling colony of polyps.

Siphonophores and chondrophores are hydrozoans that live in floating colonies. An example is the Portuguese man-o' war. It is an association of feeding, defensive, and reproductive polyps, all supported by a gas-filled float. The Portuguese man-o' war trails very powerful stinging cells in the water to catch prey.

Although most hydrozoans live in the sea, Hydra is a freshwater species. The long tentacles surround the central mouth, which is at the top of the saclike body.

Fact File

HYDROZOANS

Orders: Athecata, Thecata, Milleporina, Siphonophora, Chondrophora (about 3,000 species altogether)

Class: Hydrozoa

Phylum: Cnidaria

Where do they live?: Worldwide in all seas and oceans and occasionally in fresh water

Habitat: Seashore and seabed, on rocks, plants, and other animals; siphonophores and chondrophores found in mid water

Size: Very variable: many polyps are very small; hydroid colonies up to 6 inches (15 cm); floating siphonophores can be several feet long, including trailing tentacles

Coloration: Varies greatly: many are transparent, pinkish, brownish, or even yellowish

Diet: Small particles of food collected by the tentacles and small and medium-sized animal prey stung to death by stinging cells on the tentacles

Breeding: The medusoid phase of hydroids reproduces sexually, leading to a larval phase; many hydrozoans can reproduce by asexual budding

Status: Not known

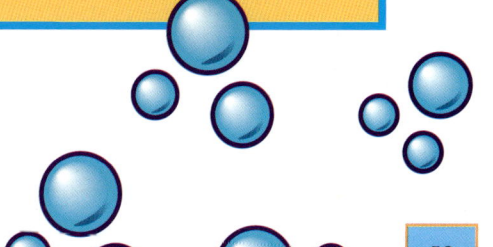

JELLYFISH

A jellyfish's graceful and often beautiful appearance, coupled with its rhythmical and languid swimming behavior, hide the danger that lurks among the deadly trailing tentacles.

INVERTEBRATES

The adult stages of jellyfish are known as medusae. They usually have umbrella- or helmet-shaped bodies, often referred to as the bell, although some species are square or box shaped. Jellyfish get their name due to the jellylike layer between the outer and inner layers of cells in their bodies. Much of this jelly is composed of water. When jellyfish are stranded on the beach, their jellylike nature is very easy to see.

Under the Umbrella

The mouth is on the underside of the umbrella and leads up into the digestive cavity that spreads throughout the interior of the bell. There is no anus in jellyfish. There are many tentacles arranged around the edge of the umbrella, and these are armed with powerful stinging cells. They are used to catch prey and can be shortened or lengthened by the jellyfish at will.

The edge of the umbrella is folded into a series of flaps. Between these flaps, and arranged rather like the position of the numbers 12, 3, 6, and 9 on a clock face, are sensory structures or balancing organs. Sometimes there are eight of these structures present, sometimes four, depending on the species.

Underneath the bell, and around the mouth, are four, often frilly oral arms, also equipped with stinging cells. They are called oral arms because they help get food into the jellyfish's mouth when it feeds. In some species, the oral arms are used to look after developing larvae.

The yellowish, frilly oral arms are clearly visible in this Australian spotted jellyfish. It feeds on plankton, fish eggs and larvae, and marine snails.

Fact File

JELLYFISH

Classes: Scyphozoa (about 200 species), Cubozoa (19 species)

Phylum: Cnidaria

Where do they live?: All seas and oceans

Habitat: Usually swimming in the water column; some live upside-down on the seabed

Size: Adults 0.5 inches–6.5 feet (13 mm–1.9 m) in diameter

Coloration: Often transparent but with many shades of color; some patterning

Diet: Invertebrates including plankton plus animals as large as fish

Breeding: Sexes in medusae are usually separate; sperms and eggs are shed via the mouth; fertilization takes place in the sea; a swimming larva gives rise to the polyp phase and develops into a strobila, from which small larval jellyfish bud off by asexual reproduction; these grow into mature medusae

Status: Unknown

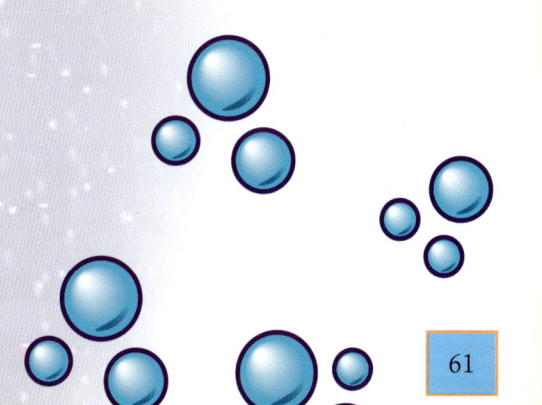

JELLYFISH

▽ *Jellyfish are efficient hunters of marine life, but many are themselves eaten by other sea creatures, including sea turtles such as the one seen here.*

Stinger in the Sea

For many people, jellyfish are known because of their stings. The stings are produced by special microscopic cells, called cnidae, found especially on the tentacles and oral arms. The cnidae contain a capsule with a coiled-up hollow filament. This is called a nematocyst. When the cnidae are stimulated by a particular chemical, or by being touched, the nematocysts instantly shoot out the coiled-up filament. Some of them penetrate the flesh of prey or predators and inject venom. Others are longer and threadlike and are used to ensnare victims.

Nematocysts are the perfect weapon for soft-bodied animals like jellyfish, that cannot grip or bite their prey. Jellyfish often break up in rough water and broken pieces of tentacle can still cause as much discomfort as whole animals if they are touched by a swimmer, for example.

DID YOU KNOW?

- Some jellyfish glow in the dark and emit flashes of light.
- A group of jellyfish with trumpet-shaped bodies—known as stalked jellyfish—spends the medusa phase attached to weeds in shallow water or rock pools.
- The upside-down jellyfish does not swim about in the water, but instead lies upside-down with its "umbrella top" touching the seabed.

Box Jellyfish

All jellyfish sting, but the stings from the box jellyfish place them among the most poisonous animals in the world. Some box jellyfish have such powerful stings that they can kill a

INVERTEBRATES

◐ *A deadly box jellyfish, or sea wasp, pulls a captured shrimp into its mouth.*

◐ *Landlocked jellyfish in a lake on the island of Palau.*

released, via the mouth, into the sea where fertilization takes place and a larva forms. The larva attaches itself to the seabed and develops into a polyp. The polyp then produces lots of tiny medusae by a process called budding. When the medusae reach a certain size they leave the polyp and swim away to grow into adult medusae, so completing the life cycle.

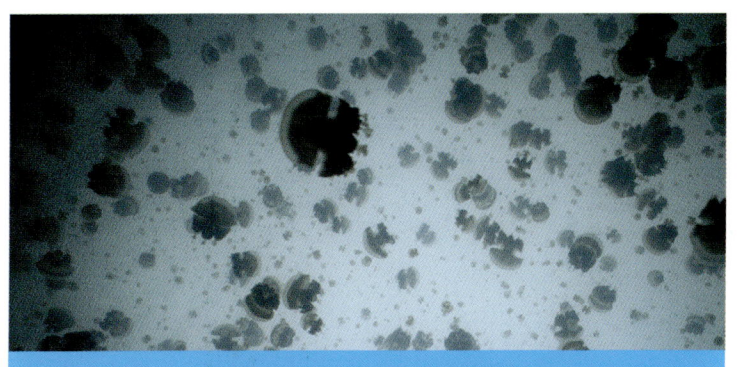

human. Divers gain some protection from the deadly stings by wearing protective clothing such as very thin nylon suits. The nematocysts cannot penetrate the material, and so cannot reach the divers' skin.

Having Young

Four reproductive organs alternate with the oral arms around the mouth of the medusa. There are separate male and female jellyfish in many species, but a few are hermaphrodites (having both male and female sex organs at the same time). The sex organs usually ripen in the spring or summer. Sperm and eggs are usually

JELLYFISH FOR DARWIN

The island of Palau in the Pacific Ocean, east of the Philippines, has about seventy seawater lakes. Water seeps to and from the sea via minute holes in the island's rock, but even the smallest animal cannot get through. About five of the lakes contain imprisoned jellyfish. Each lake contains a unique jellyfish species, different from all the others. This is similar to Charles Darwin's discovery of different finch species on different Galapagos Islands. It supports his theory of evolution in the same way, by showing that isolated species develop special adaptations to suit their particular environment.

KRILL

Looking a lot like shrimp, these tiny crustaceans are found in enormous numbers in the world's oceans, where they are one of the main food sources for many other marine creatures.

INVERTEBRATES

Krill are tiny crustaceans (animals belonging to the group that includes shrimp and crabs). Krill are found worldwide as part of the plankton, often near the surface and especially in the polar seas. They are very abundant in the Southern Ocean around Antarctica, frequently occurring in huge numbers. Krill feed on minute floating plants called phytoplankton. In turn, krill are preyed on by whales which sieve the surface waters swallowing tens of thousands of them in one gulp—up to 4 tons in one day's feeding! Different whale species are adapted to take krill of different sizes. This reduces competition between them. The main krill feeders are blue, right, and fin whales, but other animals, such as seals, penguins, and seabirds, eat them as well. Commercial fisheries have been set up to catch krill but have not really been successful.

Light in the Water

Shallow-water krill species have conspicuous eyes. In temperate and tropical waters, they respond to the amount of light in the water, rising to the surface at night when fewer predators are about. Throughout the continuous daylight of the summer at the poles they remain near the surface, however. Krill have special light-producing organs along the body, which look like lines and dots. These light up under the control of the nervous system, and the bluish glow they generate is seen by other krill and helps keep them together.

Krill feed on algae on the underside of ice in Antarctica. Their hairy legs function as a basketlike sieve to collect the microscopic plant life.

Fact File

KRILL

Order: Euphausiacea (about 90 species in 2 families)
Class: Malacostraca
Subphylum: Crustacea
Phylum: Arthropoda

Where do they live?: All seas and oceans

Habitat: Surface waters or at particular depths (according to species); not touching the seabed

Size: 1–2 inches (2.5–5 cm)

Coloration: Transparent with internal organs showing through in various colors

Diet: Marine phytoplankton, small zooplankton, and tiny food particles

Breeding: Separate sexes; adults mate while swimming; the fertilized eggs sink into deep water and hatch into a series of non-feeding, and then feeding, larvae; larvae then swim upward again to complete their development—this prevents the filter-feeding adults from eating their own young

Status: Not known, but krill numbers may have fallen by as much as four-fifths since 1970, possibly due to the shrinking of Antarctic pack ice

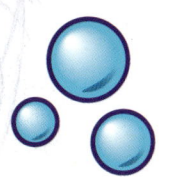

65

LANCELETS

Although they resemble eel-like fish, the humble lancelets are in fact a primitive group that are part way between those animals that do not have a backbone (invertebrates) and those that do (vertebrates).

PRIMITIVE FISH

Lancelets are small marine animals that spend much time burrowing in the seabed, although they can swim. Their narrow, fishlike body is pointed at both ends. They have a narrow dorsal (back) fin and a small, rounded tail fin. The head of a lancelet is small and has no eyes. There is a well-developed nerve cord that connects with a simple brain. The brain is not enclosed in a braincase. The mouth has no jaws or teeth, and is surrounded by sensory tentacles. The mouth leads into the pharynx or throat. Unlike fish, whose gills are in direct contact with the water, the gills of lancelets are in a cavity connected to the pharynx.

Lancelets are filter feeders. They draw water into the gills through the mouth and sieve out food particles. The particles are collected and passed along a channel to the animal's intestine. Lancelets use the gills to extract oxygen from the water at the same time.

How Backbones Evolved

The structure of a lancelet's body tells us a lot about the phylum Chordata (the group that includes vertebrate animals such as humans) and their origins. Despite their fishlike appearance and behavior, lancelets have no backbone. Instead, a stiffening rod of fibers and jelly runs from the front of the animal to the rear. This supports the body and provides muscle anchorage. This structure is an evolutionary forerunner of the spinal column found in vertebrates.

This Amphioxus shows the V-shaped pattern of the muscles of the body wall. These help the fish move along using side-to-side swimming movements.

Fact File

LANCELETS

Order: Amphioxiformes (about 25 speciesl)

Subphylum: Cephalochordata

Phylum: Chordata

Where do they live?: Worldwide in temperate and tropical seas and oceans

Habitat: Shallow seabed on gravel bottoms

Size: up to 4 inches (10 cm)

Coloration: Pink to white

Diet: Microscopic organic particles filtered from sea water

Breeding: Separate males and females; sperm and eggs released into sea water; a microscopic larva forms at fertilization, which lives in the plankton until ready to settle on the seabed and turn into a juvenile

Status: Not known

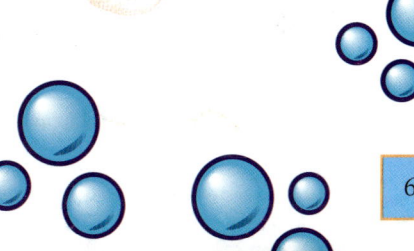

LEECHES

Many leeches are parasites—they live by sucking the blood from other animals. They can eat several times their own body weight in a single meal, and this can last them for months or even years.

INVERTEBRATES

About a quarter of leech species are predators, hunting prey such as earthworms and insect larvae. The rest bite and feed on the blood of other animals (known as hosts), clinging on while they often consume large amounts in one meal. A leech's body can stretch to accommodate its food. Leeches have sensory organs, including eyespots at the head end, which they use to detect prey. They are guided by changes in light intensity—caused by passing shadows—and scents. Their saliva has a numbing effect so that the host may be unaware of being bitten. Although leeches may seriously weaken an animal after taking a lot of its blood, they do not actually kill it in the process.

Aquatic leeches can swim, but they also move about using looping movements of their body.

Leeches in Medicine

Until the middle of the nineteenth century, leeches were used for treating a variety of ailments in parts of Europe. They were used to remove what was thought to be "bad blood." With medicinal advances, leeches lost their importance. However, by that time the medicinal leech had become almost extinct in some places. In recent years, leeches have again been used in medicine, but in different roles. For example, when leeches feed, they secrete substances that prevent the blood from clotting, and so they are useful in treatments where clotting is a risk.

These are medicinal leeches. Suckers at the front and rear of a leech's body are used for gripping onto rocks and vegetation, or for clinging to prey when feeding.

Fact File

LEECHES

Subclass: Hirudinea (about 500 species)
Class: Clitellata
Phylum: Annelida

Where do they live?: Temperate and tropical areas in fresh waters and humid environments like swamps and rainforests; some species are marine

Habitat: Freeliving, looping on soils or vegetation or swimming in search of hosts

Size: 0.4–19 inches (10mm–50 cm)

Coloration: Black, brown, green, and red, sometimes attractively patterned

Diet: Blood and animal tissue

Breeding: Hermaphrodites; individuals are males to begin with, changing to females with age; cross-fertilization of eggs by mating; embryos develop in a protective cocoon produced by the leech's body; there is no larva—embryos develop directly into juveniles

Status: Medical leech endangered, vulnerable, or rare over most of western Europe; status of other species not known

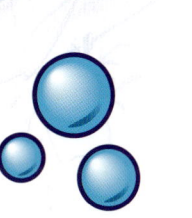

LIMPETS

Limpets are a common sight on many seashores, clinging firmly to rocks with their powerful suckers. Yet despite appearing to be fixed to the spot, they also move around in search of food.

INVERTEBRATES

Limpets are familiar residents of the rocky shore, where they may be found in great numbers. These relatives of slugs and snails live around the mid-tide level, and are regularly covered and uncovered by the sea. They feed when the tide is in, because it is easier for them to move then. When the tide ebbs they stop feeding and clamp their shells down to prevent moisture loss from their bodies. This also reduces the risks from predators such as birds and crabs. The large muscular foot also acts as a powerful sucker to grip the rocks. Experiments suggest that limpets return to the same place on the rocks at each low tide. The limpet's shell is a precise fit on its chosen bit of rock, and there may be a mark or scar where it has settled down.

Teeth on the Tongue

Limpets graze on young seaweeds. They do this using a special ribbonlike tongue which is coated with a complex array of sharp teeth. The tongue rasps backward and forward, like a strip of sandpaper, tearing the food from the rocks. It leaves characteristic marks behind. As teeth wear out at one end new ones grow at the other. Limpets are such efficient grazers that they keep the growth of algae on the middle shore in check. This helps to maintain the ecological balance of the seashore. If all of the limpets are removed from a rocky shore it can have a dramatic effect. The algae grow too vigorously because they are not being grazed.

This common limpet, on rocks in Cornwall, England, has lifted its conical shell, revealing the large muscular foot that it uses when creeping along.

Fact File

LIMPETS

Order: Archaeogastropoda (number of species unknown)
Class: Gastropoda
Phylum: Mollusca

Where do they live?: Worldwide in all seas and oceans

Habitat: Seashore and shallow seabed

Size: 0.08–5 inches (2mm–13 cm)

Coloration: Shells gray, brown, and bluish, and sometimes patterned with yellows and reds

Diet: Algae and other plant matter

Breeding: Hermaphrodite; individuals start life as males and then change into females; spawning is triggered by rough seas; fertilization occurs in sea water; a larva is formed which swims as part of the plankton before it develops into a young limpet that settles on the seabed

Status: Not known

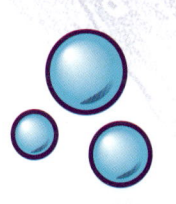

LIONFISH, SCORPIONFISH

Lionfish may not look like lions, but they can hunt just as efficiently. Scorpionfish do not look like scorpions, either, but one feature they have in common is the ability to deliver a powerful, even deadly, sting.

ADVANCED BONY FISH

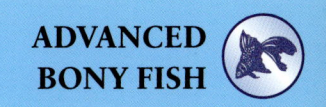

Lionfish are known by many names, some more fanciful than others. The best-known of these are: turkeyfish, tigerfish, dragonfish, butterfly cod, and scorpionfish. The last of these is a little confusing, because the name scorpionfish is usually used to describe another group of around 180 species of venomous fish in the same family.

Both lionfish and scorpionfish carry venom in glands in their fin spines, and this can be injected into would-be predators. However, these fish never use their fearsome weapons in attack, only in self-defense.

Lionfish in Action

Although they belong to the same family, lionfish and scorpionfish use different hunting techniques.

Lionfish often hunt in open water. This, of course, makes them visible to their prey. However, once they spread their large fins, tip their head slightly downward and make no apparent swimming movements, they look more like a clump of drifting seaweed than a large-mouthed hunter. They can then float slowly toward their intended prey, which never suspects it is in any danger until it is too late—by which time it has been swallowed by the lionfish.

If they are hunting close to rocks, lionfish can use their large pectoral (chest) fins to herd prey into a corner before making a lethal lunge at their victim. They can also sit and wait for prey on a ledge or by the

The body coloration and fin design help this lionfish disguise itself as seaweed as it sneaks up on prey. For protection, the spines are armed with strong poison.

Fact File

LIONFISH, SCORPIONFISH

Family: Scorpaenidae (from 200–380 species, depending on the classification used)

Order: Scorpaeniformes

Where do they live?: All tropical and temperate seas

Habitat: Mainly shallow water marine environments, although some species enter estuarine water; some species can be found in deep water as well; lionfish (e.g. *Pterois* species) often swim in open water; others (e.g. *Scorpaena* species) usually lie on the bottom

Size: From around 1.6–40 inches (4 cm–1 m)

Coloration: Varied, ranging from bold dark and light bands in some lionfish, to mottled or drab in many scorpionfish and stonefish (*Synanceia* species)

Diet: Invertebrates and fish

Breeding: Eggs are fertilized inside the female's body in most species and are later released into the water and abandoned; the eggs of some species are laid inside a jellylike "balloon"

Status: The bocaccio rockfish is listed as critically endangered; the redfish and the shortspine thornyhead are endangered; the St Helena deepwater scorpionfish or deepwater jack is vulnerable

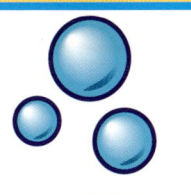

LIONFISH, SCORPIONFISH

DID YOU KNOW?

- Queensland aboriginals have a dance which they use to teach their children about the dangers of stepping on stonefish.
- Many scorpionfish have delicate, white tasty flesh that is highly rated as food, particularly in Mediterranean countries.
- The lower rays of the pectoral (chest) fin in some species are specially adapted for "walking" along the sea floor.

▲ *Like many other members of the family Scorpaenidae, the lionfish has a large mouth for snatching prey.*

▶ *Because scorpionfish lie on the bottom waiting for prey, they have an upward-facing mouth and eyes.*

entrance to a cave, where their unusual body shape makes it hard for prey to spot them.

Sitting Scorpions

Scorpionfish do not generally hunt in open water. Instead, they use a sit-and-wait technique. Being well camouflaged, many species look just like the sponge- and algae-covered sea floor that they live on.

An exception to this is the leaf scorpionfish, where the dorsal (back) fin spines and rays are much longer than in most other scorpionfish. When the fin is spread out, and the front spines are tilted forward and extend over the head, the impression created is that of a leaf, rather than a fish. This effect is reinforced by the fish's movements, which consist of side-to-side swaying like a leaf being rocked by gentle currents.

In the decoy scorpionfish, the dorsal fin has a fishlike pattern. When a potential meal approaches, the scorpionfish—which lies motionless on the bottom—flashes its dorsal fin repeatedly, fooling its unsuspecting target into thinking that the fin is a food item. However, as soon as it is within striking

ADVANCED BONY FISH

distance, the scorpionfish sucks its victim up in a single gulp.

Lethal Stones

Stonefish are often grouped in the same family as lionfish and scorpionfish (although opinions vary among scientists). Stonefish also have venomous spines. These are so dangerous that two species, the estuarine stonefish and one known simply as the stonefish, are the most venomous fish on Earth.

Stonefish are feared wherever they are found, and with good reason. At best, a sting from a stonefish is extremely painful. At worst, victims can die within a short time of being stung. This is because the venom affects nervous tissues—damaging them in the case of minor stings, or actually killing them in severe cases. The weapons a stonefish uses are awesome. They have thirteen dorsal fin spines, plus those found on the anal (belly) and pelvic (chest) fins. When threatened, the stonefish pumps venom into the puncture wounds created by the spines.

◊ *The deadly stonefish is another master of camouflage, blending in superbly among the rocks on the seabed.*

HOT WATER REMEDY

Lionfish, scorpionfish, and stonefish are not aggressive and only use their powerful venom in self-defense. Few people get stung by these fish, and when they do it is usually by accident. Nevertheless, when someone is stung, prompt action is necessary, since—in serious cases—this can be the difference between life and death.

Surprisingly, the most effective first remedy when stung is an extremely simple one: hot water. If the affected part of the victim's body is immersed in water that is as hot as can be tolerated within a few minutes of being stung, the results can be quite remarkable. The reason for this is that heat breaks down the venom and helps to neutralize it.

GLOSSARY

antenna Sensory feeler on the head of some creatures, such as lobsters and prawns
appendage Any external part of the body that is joined to the trunk, such as a whale's flipper
aquatic Living in, or relating to, water
arctic Of, or relating to, the north pole or surrounding area
asexual reproduction Reproduction that does not involve the joining of male and female sex cells

bacteria (singular: bacterium) Tiny, single-celled microorganisms that, in some cases, cause disease
baleen Thick, curtainlike substance that hangs from the upper jaw of baleen whales; filters krill out of the sea water
barbel A tentaclelike feeler near the mouth of some fish that is used for touch and taste
binary fission Asexual reproduction in which the parent cell splits into two equal parts
bioluminescence The production of light by a living organism
bivalve Type of mollusk, such as a clam, in which the shell is formed of two halves (valves) that are hinged together
brood Offspring (young) of a single birth, or clutch of eggs; also means to care for the eggs or young
budding Reproduction in which part of an organism develops into a new individual

camouflage Pattern of coloration, or body shape, that allows an animal to blend in with its surroundings
carapace Shell of a crustacean
carnivore Meat eater; animal that catches other animals for food
carrion Dead and decaying animal flesh used as food
cellulose Tough substance that makes up the cell walls of plants
chordate Animal belonging to the phylum Chordata; these animals either have a primitive or full backbone
cilium (plural: cilia) Short, beating, hairlike structure usually found on the outer surface of some cells
class Category in classification, ranking above order and below phylum (see p.78)
classification Organization by scientists of different organisms into groups (see p.78)
cnidarian Soft-bodied invertebrate animal that has stinging tentacles (for example, a jellyfish or anemone)
crustacean Invertebrate animal with paired, jointed legs and a hard outer shell (for example, water flea or shrimp)

digestion The breakdown of food into small, easily absorbed molecules in the digestive system
DNA Deoxyribonucleic acid; the molecule present in the cells of all living organisms that carries the information needed to create new life
dominant Highest-ranking
dormant Inactive and in a deep sleep, during which the animal's processes slow down

echinoderm Invertebrate animal with a spiny skin (for example, starfish or sea urchin)
echolocation Use of sound echoes by animals such as dolphins to build a picture of the surroundings
embryo Early stage in the life cycle of an organism while it is in the egg or in its mother's body
endangered species Any species that is extremely close to becoming extinct in the wild
estuarine Of an estuary; describes water that is a mixture of sea and fresh water
estuary Stretch of water where fresh water from a river mixes with sea water; estuary water is less salty than pure sea water
evolution The way in which species of living organisms slowly change over very long periods of time

extinct Any species not found in the wild for a very long time, and which is therefore thought to have disappeared forever
extinction The dying out of a species

family A category in classification that ranks above genus and below order (see p.78)
feces Expelled waste products of digestion
fertilization During sexual reproduction, the joining of a male sperm with a female egg to form an embryo
filter feeder Animal that feeds by straining tiny food particles from the water
fin Winglike or paddlelike organ attached to parts of the body of some aquatic animals that helps them move in water
flagellum (plural: flagella) Long, whiplike structure found on the cells of some organisms and used to help them move
fossil The hardened remains or imprint of an animal or plant from the past found in rock

gamete Sex cell (sperm) of a male organism or the sex cell (egg) of a female organism
gene Section of DNA that carries the code for one inherited feature
genus A category of classification for groups of closely related species (see p.78)
gestation Time an animal spends developing inside its mother (pregnancy)
gill Organ found in fish and many other aquatic animals that is used for breathing
gill chamber Part of the body where gills are located

habitat The environment in which an animal or plant usually lives or grows
hatch Break out of an egg
herbivore Plant-eating animal
hermaphrodite Animal (or plant) that has both male and female sex organs
hibernate To spend a period of time in an inactive, or dormant, sleeplike state
host Animal or plant that is preyed upon by a parasite

incubation Period during which an egg develops before hatching
intertidal Between the tides
invertebrate Animal without a backbone

krill Tiny shrimplike planktonic animal life that floats in the oceans and forms the main food of some animals such as whales

larva (plural: larvae) First stage in the life cycle of some animals after hatching
leptocephalus (plural: leptocephali) Ribbonlike, transparent larvae of an eel
ligament Elasticlike tissue that holds certain parts of an animal's body together
livebearer Animal that gives birth to fully formed young

mantle Folded tissue covering the body of mollusks; its outer layer makes the shell
medusa Swimming, usually bell-shaped, stage in the life cycle of a jellyfish
metabolism The chemical changes in living cells that provide energy for essential life processes such as growth and repair
migration Seasonal, long-distance journey by animals, such as whales, often to feed or breed
mollusk Invertebrate animal that usually lives inside a protective shell (for example, clam, sea snail, or whelk)
molt To shed or lose (for example, the carapace of a crustacean)
mucus Slimy liquid produced by the bodies of some animals and used to lubricate or protect

niche The place of an organism in a community of plants and animals
nocturnal Active during the night

nucleus (plural: nuclei) Structure found in the cell of living organisms that controls many of the activities of the cell
nutrient Food that gives an animal or plant energy to grow

omnivore Mammal that eats both plants and animals
order Category of classification ranking above family and below class (see below right)
organ Specialized group of cells in an animal's body that carry out particular tasks (for example, lungs and heart)
organism Any living thing

parasite Organism that gets its food from another living organism (the host); parasites usually harm the organism on which they feed
photosynthesis Process by which green plants make food from water and carbon dioxide using the energy of sunlight
phylum Major category of classification, above class and below kingdom (see right)
plankton Microscopic animal and plantlike life in water
polyp Tiny, anemonelike creature, usually living inside a protective, chalky cup; coral polyps form coral reefs
predator Animal that kills and eats other animals
prey Animal caught and eaten by another animal

range Geographic area within which a species usually lives

ray One of the bony rods that supports the fin of a fish
reproduction Process by which an organism produces new individuals like itself; reproduction may be sexual or asexual

scavenger Organism that eats anything it can find, living or dead (for example, some crabs)
sedentary Staying in one place; for example, barnacles attach themselves permanently to a rock or a whale
sediment Material that settles on the seabed; a mixture of tiny living organisms, sand, mud, and fragments of dead organisms
sexual reproduction Reproduction that involves the joining of male and female sex cells
shell Hard outer covering of some animals, particularly many mollusks and crustaceans
species Related organisms that resemble one another and can breed among themselves, but are not able to breed with other species
substrate Any surface upon which an organism lives (for example, the seabed or rocks)
symbiosis Relationship between two or more unrelated species of organisms in which each organism gets benefit

territory The area that an animal occupies and defends against intruders

vertebrate Animals belonging to the subphylum Vertebrata; these animals have a full backbone

zooplankton Minute invertebrate animals that form part of the plankton

---

The kingdom Animalia is subdivided into a number of categories. Shown here is the classification of the Atlantic salmon.

Category	Scientific Name	Common Name
Kingdom	Animalia	animals
Phylum	Chordata	animals with a stiffening structure in their back
Subphylum	Vertebrata	animals with a true backbone
Superclass	Gnathostomata	fish with jaws
Grade	Osteichthyes	fish with a bony skeleton
Class	Actinopterygii	fish with fins made of webs of skin and rays
Division	Teleostei	advanced bony fish
Subdivision	Euteleostei	catfish, minnows and relatives
Superorder	Protacanthopterygii	pikes, smelts and relatives
Order	Salmoniformes	salmon-like fish
Family	Salmonidae	salmon, trout, char, and relatives
Genus	*Salmo*	salmon and trout
Species	*Salmo salar*	Atlantic salmon

78

FURTHER RESOURCES

BOOKS

Beer, Amy-Jane and Derek Hall. *Marine Fish & Sea Creatures.* London: Lorenz Books, 2007.

Byatt, Andrew, Alastair Fothergill, and Martha Holmes. *Blue Planet: A Natural History of the Oceans.* New York: Dorling Kindersley, 2001.

Campbell, Andrew and John Dawes. *The New Encyclopedia of Aquatic Life.* New York: Facts On File, 2004.

Cleave, Andrew. *Seashores.* London: Hamlyn Children's Books, 1991.

Cohat, Yves and Anne Collet. *Whales: Giants of the Seas and Oceans.* New York: Abrams, 2001.

Connor, Judith. *Seashore Life on Rocky Coasts.* Monterey: Monterey Bay Aquarium, 1993.

Day, Trevor. *Exploring the Ocean (volumes 1–4).* New York: Oxford University Press, 2003.

Ellis, Richard. *Encyclopedia of the Sea.* New York: Alfred A. Knopf, 2000.

Evans, P. J. H. *Marine Mammals: Biology and Conservation.* New York: Plenum Press, 2001.

Hall, Derek and Heather Angel. *Ocean Life.* Wales: Island Books, 2008.

Hayward, Peter, Tony Nelson-Smith, and Chris Shields. *Collins Pocket Guide to the Seashores of Britain and Northern Europe.* London: HarperCollins, 1996.

Hoyt, Erich. *Creatures of the Deep: In Search of the Sea's Monsters and the World They Live In.* Toronto: Firefly, 2001.

MacQuitty, Miranda. *Shark.* London: Dorling Kindersley, 1999.

Meinkoth, N. A. *National Audubon Society Field Guide to North American Seashore Creatures.* New York: Alfred A. Knopf, 1998.

Ruppert, E., R. Fox and R. D. Barnes *Invertebrate Zoology (7th edition).* Florence, KY: Brooks/Cole, 2004.

Sprung, Julian. *Corals: A Quick Reference Guide.* Florida: Ricordea, 1999.

Stone, Lynn M. *Jellyfish.* Florida: Rourke Publishing, 2006.

Tackett, Denise Nielsen and Larry Tackett. *Reef Life: Natural History and Behaviors of Marine Fishes and Invertebrates.* Charlotte, VT: Microcosm, 2002.

Tudge, C. *The Variety of Life: A Survey and a Celebration of All the Creatures That Have Ever Lived.* Oxford: Oxford University Press, 2002.

Weinberg, Samantha. *A Fish Caught in Time: The Search for the Coelacanth.* New York: HarperCollins, 2000.

INTERNET RESOURCES

Corals
A seaworld coral site with lots of information. Very user friendly. The seaworld site also has many other interesting categories of marine life to explore.
http://www.seaworld.org/infobooks/coral/home/html

Crustaceans
Extensive information on all the major (and some minor) groups of crustaceans. Includes a simple search facility.
http://www.crustacea.net

Enchanted Learning
Check out all kinds of marine creatures, such as octopuses, clams, sharks, whales, and dolphins, as well as information about oceans and many other aspects of the natural world. Full of informative diagrams, activities, and printouts.
http://www.enchantedlearning.com

Fishbase
An amazing Web site full of information even on rare and obscure fish, with lots of references to other sources.
http://www.fishbase.org

Florida Museum of Natural History
Superb site full of pictures and information about all kinds of fish and other marine life. Includes how to become a biologist, how to avoid a shark attack, puzzles, games, and much more.
http://www.flmnh.ufl.edu/fish/

Marlin
The Marine Life Information Network for Britain and Ireland is a fascinating site providing information about sealife and conservation. With games, quizzes, virtual tours, and photographs.
http://www.marlin.ac.uk

Microbus
Click on the applications section for a tour of the microscopic life in ponds, on beaches, and inside other animals.
http://microscope-microscope.org

Mollusks
A basic introduction to this large group of mainly marine animals.
http://www.ucmp.berkeley.edu/mollusca/mollusca.html

Monterey Bay Museum
This site has an online tour to the aquarium with live-cams in various exhibits.
www.mbayaq.org

Save the Whales
Education about marine mammals and their conservation. The site provides descriptions of a variety of whales, dolphins, porpoises, and other marine mammals.
www.savethewhales.org

Zoology
A broad introduction to zoology, with lots of interesting information, plus links to other aspects of the subject, such as classification, famous zoologists, and the various branches of the science.
http://www.wikipedia.org/wiki/zoology

INDEX

Page numbers in *italic* type refer to illustrations. Page numbers in **boldface** refer to main articles on a subject.

A
Alosa vistonica (herring) 55
Amphioxus (lancelet) 66
amphipods 34, 35
anchovy 55
anglerfish 21

B
barnacles 33
blubber 33
bocaccio rockfish 73
butterfly cod 73

C
capelin 39
carp, common 27
chondrophore 59
corals
   fire 59
   reef-building 59
crabs, hermit **52–53**

D
deepwater jack 73
dragonfish 73

E
eels, freshwater **16–19**
   American 17
   elver *19*
   European *16*, 17
   glass *19*

F
fangtooths **10–11**
   common 11
   shorthorn 11
flying characin *see* hatchetfish
flying fish **12–13**
   African sailfin 13
four-eyed fish **14–15**
   finescaled 15
   large-scale 15
   Pacific 15
freshwater eels *see* eels, freshwater
frogfish **20–21**
   roughbar 21
   Sargassum 21

G
gar *see* garfish
garfish **22–23**
   alligator *22*, 23
   longnose 23
   shortnose 23
gobies **24–25**
   banded flaphead *24*
   dwarf pygmy 25
   sponge 25
   violet 25
goldfish **26–29**
   common 28
   hooded 29
   lionhead 28
   oranda 29
   shubunkin 28
   veiltail 28
gouramis **30–31**
   bubble nest *30*, 31
   croaking 31
   giant 31
   liquorice 31
gray whale *see* whales, gray
great white shark *see* sharks, great white
grunion **38–39**
guppy **40–43**
   deltatail *42*, 43
   double sword 43
   veiltail 43
   wild 43

H
hagfish **44–47**
hammerhead sharks *see* sharks, hammerhead
hatchetfish **50–51**
   common 50
   giant 51
   marbled 5
hermit crabs *see* crabs, hermit
herring **54–57**
   Atlantic 56
   giant freshwater 55
   Venezuelan 55
   West African 57
Hydra (hydrozoan) 58
hydrocoral 59
hydroid 59
hydrozoans **58–59**

J
jealous fighting fish 31

jellyfish **60–63**
   Australian spotted *60*
   box 62, 63, *63*
   landlocked *63*
   stalked 62
   upside-down 62

K
krill **64–65**

L
lampreys **44–47**
   brook *44*, 46, 47
   dwarf 46
lancelets **66–67**
leeches **68–69**
   medicinal 68, 69
leptocephali 17, 18, *18*, 19
limpets **70–71**
   common 70
lionfish **72–75**
livebearer 43

M
medusa 59, 61, 62, 63
mudskipper 25

N
nematocyst 62, 63

P
pilchard 55, 56, *56*, 57
plankton 34, 59, 65, 67
polyps 59
Portuguese man-o'-war 59
Pterois (lionfish) 73

R
redfish 73

S
sardine 55, 56, 57
Scorpaena (scorpionfish) 73
scorpionfish **72–75**
   decoy 74
   leaf 74
   St Helena deepwater 73
sea wasp 63
shads
   Alabama 55
   Macedonian 55
sharks
   great hammerhead 49
   great white **36–37**

   hammerhead **48–49**
   scalloped bonnethead 49
   scalloped hammerhead *48*, 49
   shivers 49
shortspine thornyhead 73
Siamese fighting fish 30
siphonophore 59
stings
   jellyfish 62, 63
   lionfish 75
   scorpionfish 75
   stonefish 75
stonefish 73, 75, *75*
   estuarine 75
strobila 61, 63
Synanceia (stonefish) 73

T
Tenualosa thibaudeaui (shad) 55
tigerfish 73
Trimmatom nanus (goby) 25
turkeyfish 73

W
whales
   blue 65
   calf 33, *34*
   fin 65
   gray **32–35**
   killer 35
   right 65
   watching 35, *35*

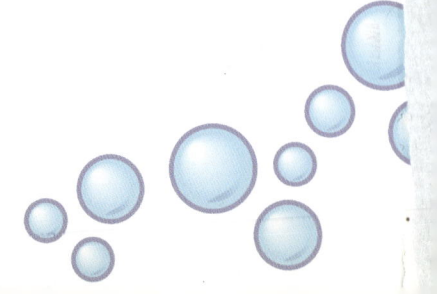